THE ULTIMATE GUIDE

TBS

WORLD CHAMPIONSHIP WRESTLING

THE ULTIMATE GUIDE

A DORLING KINDERSLEY BOOK

CONTENTS

STEVIE
RAY

INTRODUCTION

Professional wrestling has become one of the most popular spectator events in the world, and the recognized leader in professional wrestling is World Championship Wrestling (WCW). This book will serve as the ultimate guide to what makes WCW such an exciting spectacle. Every week, millions of fans tune in on television or attend live shows, watching the incredible competitors with awestruck joy. This book will allow you to go even deeper into the world of wrestling and give you the chance to learn much more about the superstars than you'd ever know just from watching the matches.

You'll read about some of the newest faces and hottest rising stars in the sport. People like Billy Kidman and Rey Mysterio, Jr., who are on the threshold of becoming megastars. Wrestlers like The Wall and The Mamalukes, who made an immediate impact upon entering the business. Also featured here are teams such as 3 Count and the Jung Dragons, who are just beginning to make their mark in WCW. They are the future of wrestling, and you can read all about them right here.

At the opposite end of the spectrum are the legends of the sport, a status that all of the newcomers wish someday to attain. What would-be superstars haven't dreamed of earning the respect of a Roddy Piper, or gaining the notoriety of an Arn Anderson? All the greats in WCW history are here, including the greatest wrestler of all time, the Nature Boy, Ric Flair, and the biggest star this sport, or any sport, has ever seen, Hulk Hogan. Only through years of blood, sweat, and tears have these men attained the accolades and championships that others only dream of, and their careers and accomplishments are covered here.

Of course, where would WCW be without all the stars of today? Each and every one of them is covered in detail for you to check out. From Sting to Lex Luger, from Bill Goldberg to Diamond Dallas Page, they are all here. We've also provided interesting facts on the superstars, including their pay-per-view debuts, titles won (and lost), and all the statistics you need to know! There's also plenty of little-known facts and stories about your favorite stars that you won't find anywhere else, except here!

World Championship Wrestling features the greatest athletes in the world, but this book is more than just a collection of bios. We've included a look at every aspect that goes into making WCW events the spectacles that they are. Every part of WCW is covered here, including a look at the diet and training methods of the stars. There are also sections on the announcers and referees, as well as an exclusive look at the beautiful women of WCW, from Kimberly to Paisley, from valets to Nitro Girls.

THE HISTORY OF WCW

To understand the present World Championship Wrestling, you need to understand its past. Although WCW, in its current form, is less than 10 years old, its lineage dates all the way back to the early 1900s; the WCW World Heavyweight Championship can be traced back to the earliest known records of world championships in the wrestling industry. WCW defended this rich history and tradition during the long war with the New World Order (nWo), and it is that same tradition that inspires the stars of WCW today. Every wrestler that ever sets foot in the ring hopes to write their own page, or even chapter, in the history book of World Championship Wrestling.

For many decades, the National Wrestling Alliance (NWA) was the governing body of professional wrestling, overseeing many small regional territories around the world. Eventually, most of the territories merged together under the banner of Jim Crockett Promotions. The flagship television program at the time was called *World Championship Wrestling*, which is still on the air to this day, now known as *WCW Saturday Night*. In November of 1988, media mogul Ted Turner purchased Jim Crockett Promotions, and began to shape it into the organization it is today, renaming the whole company World Championship Wrestling. By the summer of 1991, the NWA was a forgotten memory, and all the major championships took the WCW name.

By the middle of the 1990s, WCW was ready to show the world that it was the ultimate wrestling organization. First came a copromotion with the WCW Japanese counterpart, New Japan Pro Wrestling, for a show in North Korea on April 28, 1995. This show, headlined by New Japan's Antonio Inoki taking on WCW's Ric Flair, drew an estimated 190,000 fans, the largest crowd ever to witness a pro wrestling event. Less than four months later, on September 4, 1995, WCW debuted *Nitro*, the revolutionary live television program that has gone on to be the flagship of the promotion. The show was so incredibly popular that on May 27, 1996, after less than a year on the air, it was expanded to two hours.

The various championship titles in WCW have a history all of their own. The World Heavyweight Title dates back all the way to 1905. The World Tag Team Title was formed in the late '70s and early '80s, as several regional titles were combined to create one championship. The United States Title was initially started in the mid '70s. In the 1990s, as the company expanded, WCW added two special titles, the WCW Cruiserweight Title and the WCW Hardcore Title.

Through the history of WCW, fans have grown accustomed to seeing all the top stars in the business. While legends like Hulk Hogan and Ric Flair were on top of the industry, WCW fans saw future stars like Lex Luger and Sting gaining ground on them. Meanwhile, Booker T and Diamond Dallas Page were just getting started and were hardly the household names they are today. History shows that no one starts at the top, and now it's the new generation of WCW talent like Kidman and Vampiro that are working to become the stars of tomorrow, while stars like DDP and Booker T have acquired legendary status.

While every WCW event is special, some have been built up through time to be considered the premiere events of the year. *Starrcade* was first introduced in 1983 and has been considered the "Superbowl" of wrestling. Two years later, the *Great American Bash* was born, and has become the summertime equivalent to winter's *Starrcade*. On the same level, *Halloween Havoc* was created in 1989 and soon became the event that really set the tone for WCW. All in all, there are now twelve big events on WCW's calendar, and they are carried around the world on pay-per-view.

Of course, the easiest way to trace the history of WCW is through its incredible rise in popularity. In the '80s, you saw wrestling once or twice a week on television. The only merchandise was a few T-shirts on sale at the arenas. Now, WCW is broadcast practically every night of the week in some areas. WCW clothing is no longer just a souvenir—you're likely to see it being worn on the street every day. Of course, that's just the tip of the merchandising iceberg, one that also includes toys, CDs, video games, and even movies! WCW is everywhere, and will be for a long time to come.

RIC FLAIR

He is the greatest wrestler of all time. That is an accepted fact, repeated constantly by experts, announcers, fans, and other wrestlers. The "Nature Boy" has been a cornerstone of professional wrestling for over two decades, and his influence on the sport is immeasurable. Ric Flair, in the minds of many, IS wrestling, and with good reason. He has won more titles and wrestled in more towns than any dozen wrestlers, and he is still going strong to this day. In a sport that overuses the term "living legend," Ric Flair takes it one step further. He is an active legend, regularly showing all the greenhorns how to get the job done. Every time the theme from *2001: A Space Odyssey* blares, and he walks down that aisle "stylin' and profilin'" as only he can, school is in session for anyone that dreams of someday being a star in this business.

In the 1980s, Flair formed the original Four Horsemen along with Tully Blanchard, Ole Anderson, and Arn Anderson. Since that time, Flair has been a part of every incarnation of the group, which controlled first the NWA, then WCW, like no group before or since. The New World Order may think they're the greatest group in the history of the sport, but ask anyone who knows wrestling that question, and they'll instinctively flash four fingers!

THE DOMINATOR

You don't become the WCW World Champion by accident. Flair has dominated the championship scene in wrestling, holding more titles in more organizations than anyone who has ever laced up a pair of boots. It would take all the space in this book just to run down his history of title wins and losses. He was even the first WCW World Champion!

Sometimes called "the dirtiest player in the game," the Nature Boy isn't above, or below, bending the rules to gain a victory. Whether it's a well-timed low blow, a poke to the eyes, or a full-blown arsenal of illegal tactics, no one will ever accuse Ric Flair of being an angel. Then again, it's doubtful that anyone ever thought of Flair as anything other than a grinning devil in the ring!

RIC FLAIR

- Height: 6' 1"
- Weight: 245 lbs.
- Hometown: Charlotte, NC
- Birthday: February 25
- Debut: December 10, 1972
- Finishing maneuver: Figure-Four Leglock
- Phrase: "To be the man, you've got to beat the man! Whoooo!"
- Titles held: WCW United States Title, WCW World Heavyweight Title, WCW International World Heavyweight Title

Anytime you see a master like Flair in the ring, you know that there is no wasted effort or motion. He takes his opponents apart methodically, exploiting their weaknesses, then goes to work on the legs. After thoroughly softening them up with a series of moves and holds tailored to the specific opponent, Flair applies his trademark Figure-Four Leglock. The formula may have changed slightly over the years, but the result is still the same: victory for Flair.

Ric's Rivals

You don't go almost thirty years in this sport without developing some rivalries, and Flair has had plenty. His feud with Ricky Steamboat produced some of the most classic scientific battles you will ever see, while his wars with Terry Funk showed brutality that few can match. Flair's matches with a young Sting changed wrestling forever, as the Stinger became a major star. Of all his feuds though, the most celebrated has to be his war with Hulk Hogan over who truly is the top star in the history of this sport. It's one issue that may never be settled.

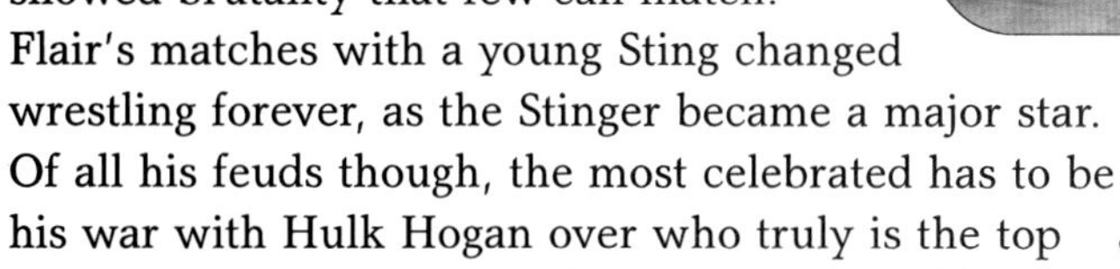

You Can't Keep a Good Man Down...

Opponents beat him, brilliant minds plot against him, but no one can keep Ric Flair down for long. He has made more comebacks than any other professional athlete, and each time he is written off, he comes back to add another world title to his résumé and laugh in the face of his detractors. Even matching him up with inferior opponents couldn't stop the Nature Boy from turning on the style. He has said: "I used to be able to have a great match with anyone, now I need someone with a pulse."

Man of Style

With his tailor-made suits and gold watches, this veteran certainly lives the lifestyle of a celebrity, as he should. When Flair talks about being a "limousine-riding, jet-flying, kiss-stealing, wheeling, dealing son-of-a-gun," it's not just bravado. He truly lives the life, and loves every minute of it. More than that, Flair loves to compete, and his love of the good life is far outpaced by his love of wrestling. Professional wrestling without Ric Flair? To most, such a thing could never exist. Ironically, one of his favorite phrases, "To be the man, you've got to beat the man," has turned out to be untrue. Because no matter how many times you beat him, you could not hope to take his place.

Crowbar

You can add another name to the list of unusual and unique competitors in the WCW roster. When David Flair was going through one of his "unstable" phases, he started carrying a crowbar into the ring. A few weeks later he had a tag team partner. His name? Crowbar. However, this Crowbar is far more effective than a piece of metal, although he often brandishes a lead pipe in the ring. One of the fastest rising stars in World Championship Wrestling, Crowbar has no fear inside the ropes, often putting his body on the line with spectacular maneuvers and suicidal dives. Obviously well-schooled in the fundamentals of the sport, Crowbar can also brawl, match power, or soar across the ring, depending upon the situation he finds himself in. He is a complete wrestler.

Just when Crowbar was really starting to make strides in WCW, his career took an unexpected turn after one of the most horrific events in WCW history. During an edition of *WCW Thunder*, in a match against The Wall, Crowbar was choke-slammed off the second rope, through the announcers' table, and onto the concrete floor. The impact was enough to send Crowbar to the hospital and caused him to miss quite a bit of action.

Crowbar

- Height: 6' 1"
- Weight: 230 lbs.
- Hometown: Rutherford, NJ
- Birthday: March 4
- Debut: January 1992
- Finishing maneuver: Inverted DDT
- Phrase: "Ladies and gentlemen, this will be a battle of epic proportions."
- Titles held: WCW World Tag Team Title

With David Flair

No one is quite clear how David Flair and Crowbar got together, but they certainly have made an effective team, already holding the WCW World Tag Team Title after conquering a field of far more established teams for the straps. While you can criticize their style—they prefer to joke around rather than wrestle during matches—they at least have the courage to take on all comers. In fact, some would say they don't care who their opponents are, as long as they get to have fun and bash skulls!

Mad as a Hatter?

The one thing that Crowbar seems to be missing is his sanity. After all, what kind of madman storms a wedding reception, knowing full well the Mammalukes are in attendance and will be looking for revenge? Crowbar went even further, teaming up with Flair to take on the Italians at their specialty, a Sicilian stretcher match. Perhaps Crowbar is only pretending to be crazy. After all, there have been rumors that he actually has a degree in physical therapy, and on his occasional stints at the microphone he comes across as a well-read, intelligent young man. But then you see that his best friends are David Flair and Daffney, and you go right back to thinking that while he may be talented and intelligent, he's got to be at least a few cards short of a full deck!

David Flair

It's not easy being the son of the greatest wrestler ever to lace up a pair of boots. For David Flair, it was definitely not easy, and the pressure he felt upon entering the sport may have scarred him for life. As the son of Ric Flair, David not only inherited his father's name, but his enemies as well. Then to make matters worse, he became a pawn used to weaken the Nature Boy. Ric Flair responded in kind, using his power as the then WCW president to punish his own flesh and blood. It all proved to be a little too much for the youngster, and he snapped.

A Woman You Can Trust?

After being used and lied to by women, David finally found someone he could trust in Daffney. A devoted David Flair fan, she used to hold one person *Nitro* parties, where her devotion to David more resembled hero worship. Once they met it was love, and they have had no problems demonstrating their love in front of everyone during WCW television, often rolling playfully around on the mat while engaged in a liplock!

David Flair

- **Height: 6' 1"**
- **Weight: 177 lbs.**
- **Hometown: Charlotte, NC**
- **Debut: 1999**
- **Finishing maneuver: Crowbar to the head**
- **Titles held: WCW United States Title, WCW World Tag Team Title**

Like Father, Like Son

The greatest act of nepotism ever in wrestling took place on July 5, 1999, when WCW President Ric Flair stripped Scot Steiner of the WCW United States Title and simply gave it to his son. It made David a marked man, and if not for Flair and Arn Anderson constantly protecting David, he wouldn't have lasted a day as champion. By the time his reign was over, David was battered, bruised, and adamant that he was not going to let that happen again!

His Own Man

Now the pressures of being the son of Ric Flair are gone. David Flair is his own man. Perhaps that should be phrased a "scary man." With his cohorts Crowbar and Daffney, David now walks around as if he were in a trance, save for brief periods where he acts goofier than a cartoon character. He has also taken to carrying around a crowbar, which he uses to destroy his opponents. He has been surprisingly successful, winning the WCW World Tag Team Title, although who knows if David even realizes the importance of it. Looking like he hasn't had a good night's sleep in months, perhaps David will one day take a long nap, only to wake up and think his whole career thus far was only a dream.

CHICAGO
BLACKHAWKS

NISSAN

KIDMAN

His finishing move is called the Shooting Star Press, but while shooting stars soon burn out, Billy Kidman's star will continue to shine brightly for years to come. He is the epitome of the young, hungry talent looking to take his place among the top wrestlers of WCW. Experts predicted big things for Kidman from the start, and after a rough period early on, he is now well on his way to fulfilling those expectations. Kidman has already held a handful of titles and is on the hunt to add more, as his reputation continues to grow.

One of Kidman's favorite outside-the-ring activities is taping the backstage happenings at WCW events with his video camera, which he calls the KidCam. While it's usually just used for harmless fun, it has gotten into the wrong hands on occasion and caught several WCW stars in rather embarrassing situations. Still, fans can't wait to see what the KidCam will catch next!

A SURE THING

Kidman is still a baby in professional wrestling terms and has years of growing before he reaches his peak. Perhaps that is what is truly remarkable about this athlete. He is already a superstar and still has so much time to improve and perfect his game. Given time and room to grow, he will be remarkable. Wrestlers like Ric Flair and Sting weren't made overnight, they took their lumps on the way to the top, and no doubt Kidman will as well. But you just get the feeling that no matter what the obstacle, he will succeed. If you were to bet on any one wrestler to fulfill his career potential, place your money on Billy Kidman.

FUTURE STAR

What does the future hold for this young star? Will he return to the cruiserweight division, where he has had so much success? Perhaps he will pursue the WCW United States Title or even the WCW World Heavyweight Championship. Regardless of which goal he chooses, it can be guaranteed that Kidman will continue to provide some of the best action in WCW.

Billy Kidman is one of the few wrestlers to master the difficult Shooting Star Press. This maneuver is a backward flip from the top rope into a splash, and most men, even aerial specialists, won't dare attempt it. Japanese legend Jushin Liger, who invented the move, doesn't even use it anymore! It's a dangerous move to perform in the ring, and it's downright scary to see. On occasion, Kidman performs it from the top rope to the floor.

Torrie Wilson

Want to know why every wrestler in WCW is envious of Billy Kidman? Two words: Torrie Wilson. This goddess accompanies Billy everywhere, and you can see what an inspiration she would be to have in your corner. Wouldn't you fight just a little bit harder if you had the lovely Torrie to impress? I guess now we know the real reason he always has that camera around! And who can blame him?

Juventud Feud

With the possible exception of Rey Mysterio Jr., no cruiserweight champion has garnered as much attention and lent such prestige to the title as Kidman. His feud with Juventud Guerrera over the strap is still talked about by fans of the high-flying lucha style, and in the minds of many, it was the feud of the year for 1998. One can only imagine the classic fights that these two young lions will have in the years to come.

Kidman

- Height: 5' 11"
- Weight: 195 lbs.
- Hometown: Allentown, PA
- Birthday: May 11
- Debut: 1994
- Finishing mancuvcr: Shooting Star Press
- Titles held: WCW World Cruiserweight Title, WCW World Tag Team Title

Tag Team Titan

Kidman has excelled in tag team competition and has won the WCW World Tag Team Title on two occasions with separate partners, once each with Rey Mysterio Jr. and Konnan. Kidman can adapt to any partner, but not all his teams have achieved such success. More than a few of his combos, most notably his teaming with Vampiro, have led to one-on-one confrontations between the former partners.

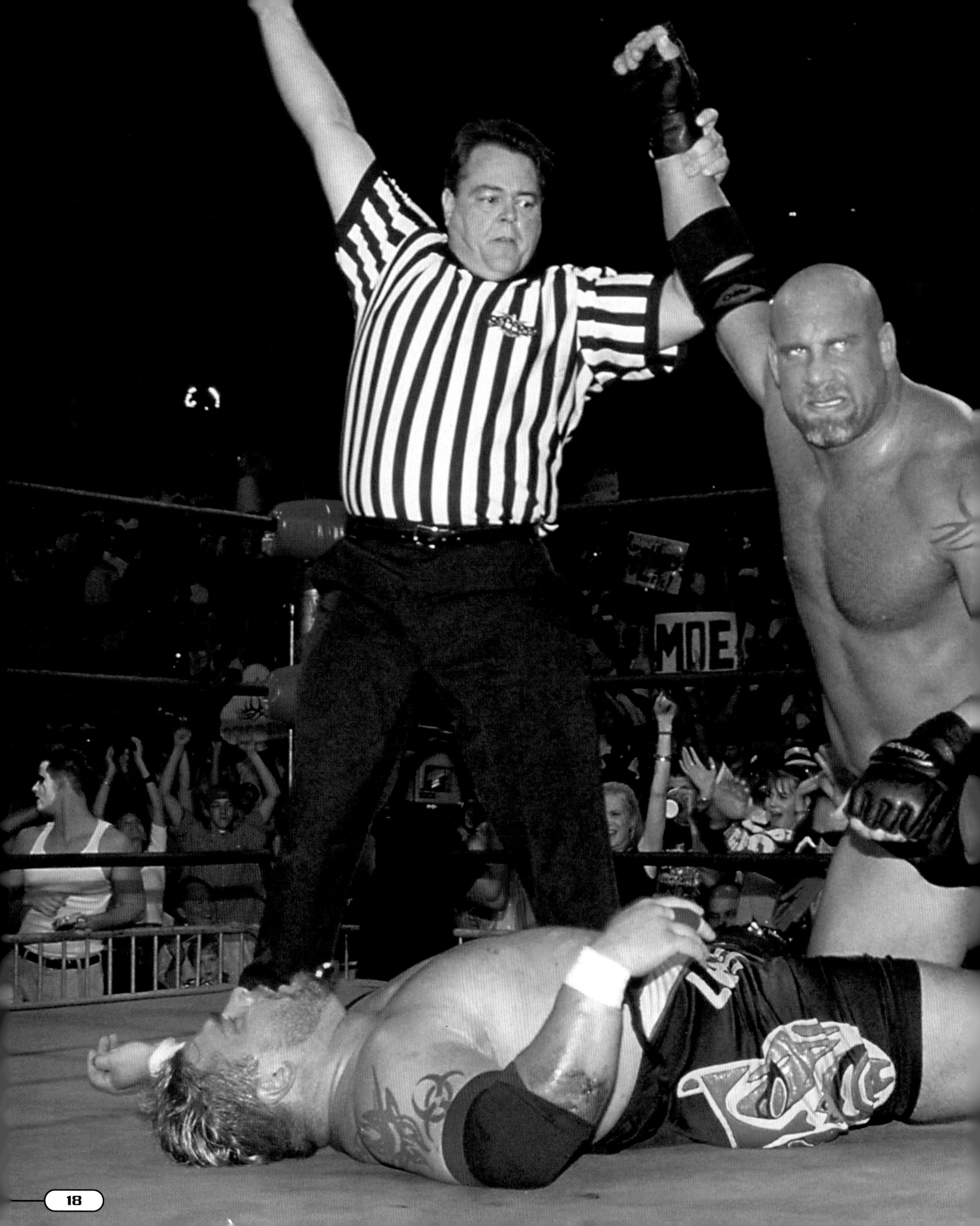
MOE

HEAVYWEIGHT

The top prize in wrestling is the WCW World Heavyweight Title. Tracing its roots back to 1905, this championship grew out of the old NWA title and evolved into its present form, with Ric Flair becoming the first WCW World Heavyweight Champion in 1991. Since then, only the elite, from Lex Luger to Bill Goldberg, have held the belt. Some wrestlers, like Hulk Hogan, Sting, Kevin Nash, and Diamond Dallas Page, have been fortunate enough to hold the title more than once. This is the pinnacle of the profession, and once you've been there, no one can ever take the achievement away from you. For as long as you possess the belt, you are the best professional wrestler in the world.

KANYON

Just to annoy him, the fans of WCW will shout out "everybody" when Kanyon asks "Who's better than Kanyon?" Chris Kanyon is one of the most versatile wrestlers in WCW and is a true student of his craft, constantly looking for new styles to incorporate into his own. Tall and lanky in build, he uses his tremendous reach advantage to overwhelm his opponents, while they are unable to apply their own holds and maneuvers. With such tremendous skills, Kanyon appears to have a bright future in the sport. For him, though, that future cannot come fast enough. Instead of just relying on his formidable assets, he chooses to take shortcuts in the ring. Always taking every possible advantage of a situation, Kanyon looks to his allies for assistance and has no qualms about using foreign objects to gain an easier victory. Recently, he has become known as "Positively Kanyon."

WCW announcer Mike Tenay has dubbed Kanyon the "Innovator of Offense" for his incredible arsenal of maneuvers, and the name certainly fits. Kanyon seems to come up with new holds on a whim, as if they flow naturally from him. No matter what situation he finds himself in during a match, Kanyon will pull out a move, usually one that has never been seen before and bring the match back over in his favor.

CHAMP

Amazingly, Kanyon's first title in WCW came as a result of his losing a match! As a replacement tag team partner, he made sure that his opponents, Diamond Dallas Page and Bam Bam Bigelow, won the match and the titles. Immediately following the bout, the world learned that Kanyon was in cahoots with Page and Bigelow all along, and their alliance, the Triad, would defend the belts together. The alliance didn't last long, but it did make Kanyon a champion!

Experts agree that Chris Kanyon has all the tools needed to go far in wrestling. Most of those same experts also agree that his biggest weakness is his arrogance. He truly thinks that no one is better than he is, and that often causes him to underestimate opponents. Kanyon will someday learn that a little humility can take him a long way.

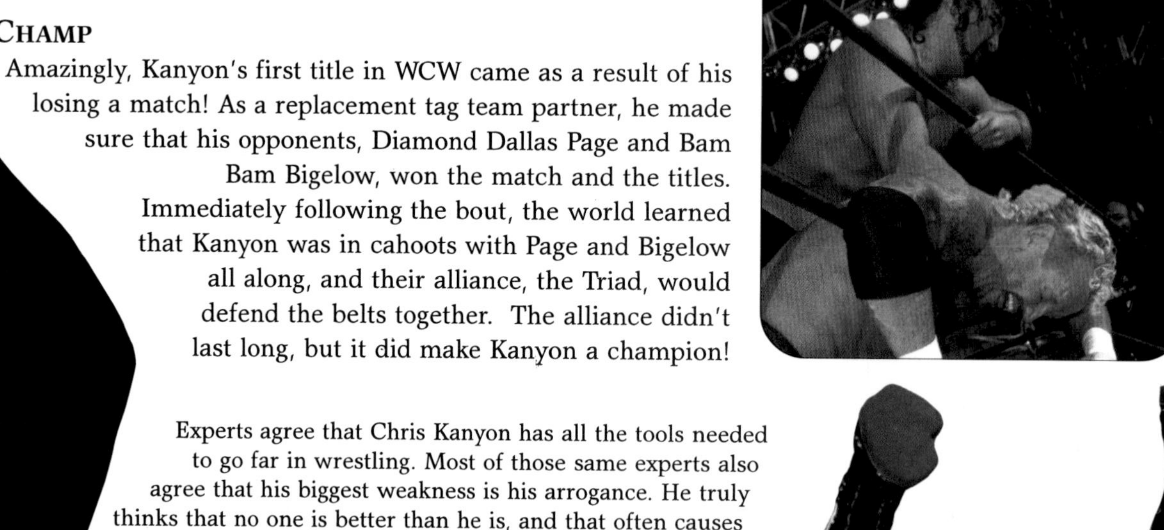

KANYON
- Height: 6' 3"
- Weight: 270 lbs.
- Hometown: Queens, NY
- Debut: 1995
- Finishing maneuver: That's a Wrap
- Phrase: "Who's better than Kanyon?"
- Titles held: WCW World Tag Team Title

Curt Hennig

Some wrestlers claim to be flawless, but very few come as close as Curt Hennig to achieving that boast. One of the best all-around competitors this business has ever produced, Hennig has the technical ability to go toe to toe with all-time greats like Ric Flair and Bret Hart, but also has the attitude to slap the taste from the mouths of young guns hoping to make their reputations in the ring with him. Some would say Hennig is arrogant, and while that is true to an extent, his bragging is always based on real achievements, not empty boasts.

Hennig is one of many second generation stars in wrestling, but unlike most, he has far exceeded the accomplishments of his father, and his dad couldn't be more proud. Larry "The Ax" Hennig passed his love and knowledge of wrestling to his son, as well as handing down a unique family heirloom, the "Ax Attack" clothesline, which Hennig still employs, knocking the heads off opponent after opponent!

To Boldly Go

A former WCW United States and World Tag Team Champion, Hennig is no stranger to the gold and remains a continuous threat to other title holders. Bold to a fault, Hennig will openly challenge anyone at anytime and has often looked stars like Goldberg and Sting right in the eye without blinking, before taking them to their limits on the mat. Hennig will chop anyone down to size, stretch them out on the mat, and slap them around before putting them away with a perfectly executed Hennigplex. Whether part of a group or on his own, Hennig is equally effective, as his strength lies not in numbers, but in his own ability.

Hennig has proclaimed himself "Minnesota's greatest athlete," and it would be hard to argue with that. Of course, there is one person who definitely disagrees, and we're not talking about football or baseball players. Ric Flair was born and raised in Minneapolis, and certainly believes that he, not Hennig, is the best the Twin Cities ever produced.

Curt Hennig
- Height: 6' 3"
- Weight: 262 lbs.
- Hometown: Minneapolis, MN
- Debut 1979
- Birthday: March 28
- Finishing maneuver: Hennig Plex
- Phrase: "I don't like to say I told you so, but... I told you so."
- Titles held: WCW World Tag Team Title, WCW United States Title

Goldberg

He is the fastest rising star in the history of professional wrestling, acheiving more in his first two years than most wrestlers will in a lifetime. WCW announcer Bobby "The Brain" Heenan dubs him, simply, "The Man." His name is Goldberg, and he is truly an unstoppable force. He has racked up victory after victory, working his way up the WCW ranks and rarely uttering a word. When he does speak, it's only to request a new opponent with his trademark phrase "Who's next?" Before he even reached his first anniversary as a wrestler, he defeated Hulk Hogan (an incredible feat in itself) and won the WCW World Heavyweight Title, becoming the only man ever to hold the World and United States titles simultaneously (he had destroyed Raven to win the US title three months earlier). Goldberg was later cheated out of the heavyweight title, but he remains one of the most powerful forces in the sport.

Goldberg's first love was the gridiron. In fact, before entering WCW, Goldberg played for the Atlanta Falcons, which was the only thing anyone knew about him in those early days, since he refused to give interviews. He preferred to let his actions in the ring speak for him—and boy did they ever!

The Rise of Man

When Goldberg quietly made his debut in September 1997 with a quick victory, no one could have guessed the impact he would have on the sport. He went on to have an incredible undefeated streak and was in fact the first ever WCW World Champion to win the title with an unblemished record. When he was finally defeated by Kevin Nash in December 1998, the other Outsider, Scott Hall, had to intervene with a stun gun to stop "The Man"!

Finishing Moves

He prefers to handle matters his own way and that usually involves the wrestling equivalent of a one-two punch that even Mike Tyson would fear. First, Goldberg flattens his opponent with the Spear, a devastating tackle where he rams his shoulder into the poor guy's midsection, driving him into the mat. Then "The Man" lifts his helpless adversary into the Jackhammer, a vertical suplex followed by a powerslam that sees the victim sandwiched between the mat and Goldberg. From there, a three count, and it's another Goldberg victory!

The Man

When he emerges from the sparks of his pyrotechnic entrance, breathing smoke, he comes to the ring with purpose. He smashes his opponents utterly, often in less than three minutes. With his snarling demeanor and aggressive attitude in the ring, you might be surprised to know that outside the squared circle, Bill Goldberg is an animal lover and is particularly fond of cats. He devotes his rare free time to animal causes and charities. He's a real pussycat when playing with his furry friends, but you try telling that to the opponents he's mopped up the ring with!

Goldberg

- **Height: 6' 3"**
- **Weight: 285 lbs.**
- **Hometown: Tulsa, Oklahoma**
- **Birthday: December 27**
- **Debut: September 1997**
- **Finishing maneuver: Spear/Jackhammer**
- **Titles held: WCW United States Heavyweight Title, WCW World Heavyweight Title**

While most newcomers to the sport rarely get to wrestle with the superstars, Goldberg's popularity with the fans demanded that he be put in the ring with the very best. In only two short years he's wrestled a who's who of the business, including Scott Hall, Curt Hennig, Diamond Dallas Page, Bam Bam Bigelow, Ric Flair, and Sid Vicious.

Hulkmania

July 6, 1998 will always be remembered as one of the greatest days in WCW history. The undefeated Goldberg not only vanquished Scott Hall, but also beat the legendary Hollywood Hulk Hogan for the WCW World Title. The event occurred during a live edition of WCW Monday *Nitro* at the Georgia Dome in Atlanta. Nearly 42,000 fans exploded with joy as "The Man" defeated Hogan with his trademark Spear and Jackhammer.

CRUISERWEIGHT

In 1996, with the mass rise of high-flying lucha libre stars and smaller mat technicians, WCW created the World Cruiserweight Championship for wrestlers who weighed under 230 lbs. This soon proved to be a tremendously coveted title, and the competition for it was always fast and furious. Wrestlers from Japan and Mexico, where the cruiserweight division is very popular, have flooded WCW to take a crack at the title. Rey Mysterio Jr., Billy Kidman, Juventud Guerrera, and The Artist are just a few of the incredible talents to claim this gold.

Rey Mysterio Jr.

He is not the largest wrestler in World Championship Wrestling—female wrestler Madusa actually outweighs him and is taller than he is. However, if you were to judge a man by the size of his heart, Rey Mysterio Jr. towers over everyone. WCW's "Flying Fury" is, pound-for-pound, probably the best wrestler in the world, and certainly the most innovative. His daring, high-risk offense has revolutionized not only the cruiserweight division, but all of wrestling.

Still in his 20s, Mysterio is actually a seasoned veteran, having made his debut in Mexico when he was only 16 years old! He even used to do his homework in the locker room while waiting for his match!

It may surprise many fans to know that Rey Mysterio Sr. is not Rey Jr.'s father, but actually his uncle. Wrestling for many years as Rey Mysterio, he bestowed the name upon his nephew when he realized the youngster's desire to carry on the family tradition between the ropes. He even allowed Rey Jr. to wear the same mask, which is a great honor in Mexican wrestling tradition.

High-Flying Champ

A multiple champion, Mysterio has taken on and defeated the best in the high-flying cruiserweight segment of WCW. From longtime rivals Psychosis and Juventud Guerrera, to more traditional grapplers like Lane and Billy Kidman, Mysterio's bouts have ranked consistently high among "Match of the Year" ballots throughout his WCW tenure. Not satisfied with that, he even crossed into the heavyweight division against the big boys of WCW.

Rey Mysterio Jr.

- Height: 5' 3"
- Weight: 140 lbs.
- Hometown: San Diego, CA
- Birthday: December 12
- Debut: 1991
- Finishing maneuver: Huracanrana
- Phrase: "Where my dogs at?"
- Titles held: WCW Cruiserweight Title, WCW World Tag Team Title

In the 1980s, diving off the top rope was considered high-risk. In the 1990s, moonsaults and flying huracanranas became the norm, thanks to Mysterio. As WCW moves into a new millennium, wrestlers are constantly looking to imitate the unique maneuvers that Rey has introduced. The scary part is, he's just getting started.

When Mysterio was forced to remove his mask after a tag team loss to Kevin Nash, many thought he might retire, disgraced. Nash thought he had ended Rey's career, but he had actually lit a new fire under him. After the incident with Nash, Mysterio demanded a single match against the Outsider, and most experts started to make funeral arrangements for Rey.

David against Goliath

Mysterio proved the experts wrong and flew around Nash, keeping him off balance until he could tie him up in a victory roll, get the pin, and earn his Giant Killer reputation! While his victories over noted big men like Bam Bam Bigelow have helped him keep the "Giant Killer" nickname, Rey truly shines in the category he helped create, the cruiserweight division.

High-flying, High-risk

When you employ the type of high-risk offense that Mysterio does, you are bound to incur injuries. Unfortunately, Mysterio has missed ring time on several occasions due to hurting his knees. An occupational hazard, Mysterio takes it in stride and refuses to change his style.

Loyal Man

Fiercely loyal, Rey Mysterio Jr. has always stayed true to WCW, despite being given offers to join the nWo. Even when his mentor Konnan joined the outlaw organization, Mysterio stayed, even though it often meant fighting two, three, or even four men by himself.

FOODS
rainbow

MONDAY
NITRO

Lt. Loco

Second generation stars have never had it easy in wrestling. Working your way up from rookie to main eventer is hard enough, but to do it in the shadow of a famous wrestling father makes it even tougher. Well, how about his three famous wrestling uncles as well? And they just happened to be the most famous wrestling family in Mexico? The pressure nearly drove young Chavo Guerrero crazy! After being fired from WCW, Chavo teamed up with a group called the Misfits in Action, and returned to WCW, univited. Now with the fitting name Lt. Loco, he has found real success and won the WCW Cruiserweight Title.

Lt. Loco
- Height: 5' 10"
- Weight: 210 lbs.
- Hometown: El Paso, TX
- Debut: May 1994
- Finishing maneuver: Swinging DDT
- Phrase: "Here's Chavo!"

Juventud Guerrera

Juventud Guerrera's name means "Youth Warrior," and it is the perfect title for this incredible superstar. A big star in Mexico, where lucha libre (the Mexican form of pro wrestling) is hugely popular, he has translated his success south of the border into an incredible run here in WCW, becoming a main feature of the fast-paced cruiserweight division. One of the few luchadores to blend successfully North American catch-as-catch-can grappling with the aerial assault popular in Mexico, Guererra, along with cohorts Rey Mysterio Jr., La Parka, and Psychosis, have introduced a whole new facet of the game into WCW, and their influence can be seen in the styles of many newcomers to the sport.

Employing such a high-risk style can sometimes take a heavy toll, and Juventud has suffered injuries as a result of his insistence on taking chances in the ring. Still, his competitive spirit always brings him back to the fray, and he sees each match as a new challenge. One challenge that came easy for Juventud was finding a way for a US audience to accept him. He did this by picking up a microphone and letting his natural charm shine through.

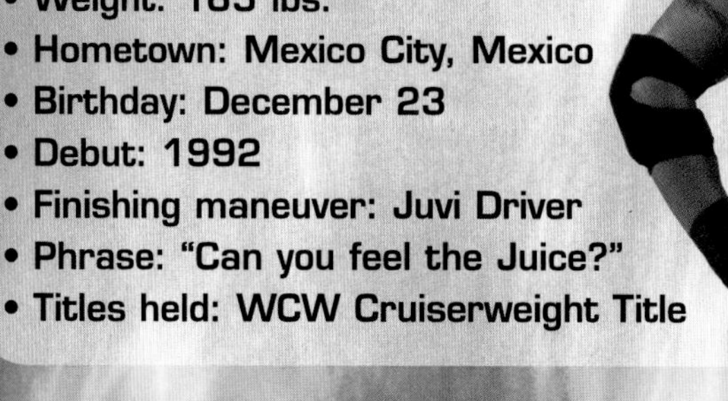

Juventud Guerrera
- Height: 5' 5"
- Weight: 165 lbs.
- Hometown: Mexico City, Mexico
- Birthday: December 23
- Debut: 1992
- Finishing maneuver: Juvi Driver
- Phrase: "Can you feel the Juice?"
- Titles held: WCW Cruiserweight Title

Harris Brothers

At 6′ 5″ and 280 pounds, one Harris brother is scary enough. Have two of them staring you down, and most tough guys start shaking in their boots as if they were in an earthquake. And earthquake is a good word to associate with these brothers, as the havoc they wreak in the squared circle is like that of a natural disaster. Few things shake the ground like their devastating H-Bomb finisher! Ron and Don Harris are positively brutal in the ring, and they become even more brutal when they have money waved under their noses. Make no mistake about it, these guns are for hire, willing to take out anybody for the chance to line their pockets with green. If you do decide to hire these brutes, you better make sure the check doesn't bounce!

When the Harris brothers first entered World Championship Wrestling, they were immediately taken out of the ring and made bodyguards to the "Powers That Be." Forced to shave their goatees and dress in suits, they were billed as Creative Control, Patrick and Gerald. As hitmen for the powers, they often stormed the ring to take care of anyone who wasn't towing the company line.

Family Bonding

Their greedy tendencies aside, this is one awesome tag team. Very few men their size have the speed and agility of these identical twins. Whether it's in a barroom brawl or a traditional tag team match, the Harris brothers are right at home—they'll even take singles matches. These two toughs have been grappling each other since they were in the womb! But don't expect to see one fight the other in the ring though—they get far more pleasure from trashing people together.

Trading Places

The Harris brothers go into each tag team match with an advantage none of their opponents have. Nope, we're not talking about their natural brotherly instinct for working together, although they certainly have that. When these two are teaming, one brother can replace the other behind the referee's back, and never get caught! Because they look exactly the same, no official can tell which brother broke the rules.

There may never be a purer tag team finisher than the Harris H-Bomb. After softening up an opponent with their other trademark move, the double boot to the face, the brothers whip their opponent into the ropes and catch him on the rebound. After lifting him over seven feet into the air, the brothers then throw him to the canvas in a modified version of the powerbomb. The most devastating aspect of the maneuver is that an opponent doesn't need to be weakened, he can be totally fresh, and still not kickout after being dropped in an H-Bomb.

The Harris Brothers

- Ron and Don Harris
- Height: Ron 6′ 5″; Don 6′ 4″
- Weight: 280 lbs. (both)
- Hometown: Nashville, TN (both)
- Birthday: October 23 (both)
- Debut: 1988 (both)
- Titles held: WCW World Tag Team Title

Leglock

The legs are a major target for attack, and wrestlers like Ric Flair and Sting, who use leglock submission holds, are always looking to get an opponent off his feet and work on the "wheels." Wrestlers often use a single-leg takedown, which is simply grabbing the opponent's leg and tripping him, and then try to apply a spinning toehold or drive their own knee into the adversary's leg to weaken him. The swifter wrestler may use a drop toehold to snare their opponent's leg. With this move, you drop to the mat, entwine your leg with that of your rival, and force him to fall forward onto his face.

3 Count

Throughout the history of entertainment, teen idols have always attracted their share of fans. With their boyish good looks, tremendous physiques, and trendy clothing, the members of 3 Count are the perfect poster boys to send teenage hearts racing. But then they open their mouths, and the image comes crashing down to earth like a missed moonsault. Convinced they are the next boy band to storm the charts, 3 Count's musical ability leaves a lot to be desired. If you want a clue as to how bad their singing really is, without actually subjecting yourself to listening to it, just consider the fact that, other than WCW announcer Mark Madden, no one admits to enjoying the noise these three make!

3 Count, hardcore? It's hard to believe, but this trio of pretty boys have actually laid claim to the WCW Hardcore Title. Former champion Brian Knobs, certainly not a fan of their music, challenged all three members in a handicap hardcore bout and was seemingly on his way to victory, flooring all three of them with trash cans and wooden crutches. But a miscue by Knobs saw him end up on his back, with all three members piling on top!

High Flyers

With its members' diminutive bodyweights, 3 Count is tailor-made for the cruiserweight division, but still comes up short against most other opposition. To make up for this, they incorporate a great deal of risky moves into their arsenal. It's not unusual to see them throw an opponent to the floor, sail over or off the top rope, and hit him with somersault sentons and twisting planchas. Obviously fans of the lucha libre style, they've combined the suicidal dives with sound technical mat wrestling to make them well-balanced competitors.

What they lack in singing ability, 3 Count more than make up for in the ring. These youngsters have done nothing but impress, putting their bodies on the line with high-risk offensives that might have you mistaking them for unmasked luchadores. Over time, it is hoped that they will learn that their future lies between the ropes, and not on the cover of a teen magazine!

3 Count

- Shannon, Shane, and Evan
- Height: Shannon 5' 8"; Shane 6'; Evan 5' 11"
- Weight: Shannon 175 lbs.; Shane 202 lbs.; Evan 204 lbs.
- Debut: As 3 Count—1999
- Phrase: "Thank you for supporting 3 Count!"
- Titles held: WCW Hardcore Title

JUNG DRAGONS

One of the most exciting trios ever to enter World Championship Wrestling, the Jung Dragons' combination of high-flying maneuvers and solid mat work makes them destined to claim championship gold. Kaz Hayashi, Jaime Son, and Yang are three cruiserweights who have pooled their talents to show that the whole can be greater than the sum of its impressive parts. By watching each others' backs, the Jung Dragons are every bit as effective in singles and traditional tag team bouts as they are in six-man tag team matches, where their amazing teamwork makes them almost unbeatable.

JUNG DRAGONS
Kaz Hayashi, Jamie-San, Yang
- **Height: Kaz 5' 9"; Jamie-San 5' 10"; Yang 5' 11"**
- **Weight: Kaz 190 lbs.; Jamie-San 215 lbs.; Yang 210 lbs.**
- **Hometown: Tokyo, Japan**
- **Debut: Kaz 1992; Jamie-San 1998; Yang 1997**

Although all businesslike in the ring, the Jung Dragons occasionally show that they have a sharp sense of humor. They once ambushed 3 Count and stole the floor discs the boys use for dance numbers when singing. The following week, the Dragons came on with the discs and sang 3 Counts' song, but in Japanese!

3 Count were not flattered by the Dragons' imitation on national television, and the result was a feud that saw six stars of the future engage in some tremendous battles.

IMPATIENT TRIO

Kaz Hayashi, Jamie-San, and Yang definitely have all the in-ring ability necessary to become stars, but they are in a rush to get there. As a result, they have been known to bend and sometimes break the rules in order to attain victory. In singles competition, it's not unusual for two of the Dragons to come to ringside and one to hop on the ring apron, distracting the referee. Meanwhile, the other will enter the ring on the opposite side and help the third Dragon destroy his opponent!

ORIENTAL FLAVOR

Kaz Hayashi, the acknowledged leader of the trio, is probably an even bigger star in his native Japan. Every year, Kaz returns to his homeland to compete in a tournament of the best cruiserweights and light heavyweights in the world and always makes a strong showing. Kaz and his partners have definitely incorporated the Japanese style into the often Mexican-influenced cruiserweight division, creating another aspect that makes that division so thrilling. Before their time is done, it will be no surprise to anyone if all three members of the Jung Dragons take a turn at being the WCW Cruiserweight Champion.

LEGG
MASON
NITRO

SETTING UP

There's a lot of preparation that goes into putting on a WCW event, and we're not just talking about the wrestlers. A huge crew puts in a hard day's work before the first bell even rings. There are rings to be built, lights and pyrotechnics to set up, sound equipment to be tested, and a lineup sheet to be constructed. The workload is even heavier when setting up one of the many live televized events WCW puts on every week. In those cases, especially, there is no room for error. Can you imagine if the ring collapsed in the middle of *Nitro*? Or how about if the lights went out in the middle of a pay-per-view event, and fans around the world were greeted with darkness on their screens? The process that goes into setting the stage for the ring wars is every bit as important as the action that takes place in the matches. It is a rarely discussed topic among wrestling fans, but the men and women that set everything up deserve a lot of credit for the success of WCW. Without them, the wrestlers would be fighting in the dark, without a ring!

Early in the morning, at an empty arena, the trucks pull up, and the activity begins. The first thing that needs to be set up, appropriately enough, is the ring. First, the steel beams and cables that connect the four ring posts are arranged on the floor, then the skeleton of the ring is erected. This is followed by layering down plywood across the weblike steel structure, followed by a layer of carpeting. Over that goes the canvas mat which the wrestlers will slam themselves into all night. Finally, the turnbuckles are connected, and the ring ropes set up. From here, the ropes are tightened, and the ring is tested, to make sure it can withstand the abuse it will take over the course of the evening.

The technical experts are always hard at work at WCW events, setting up an array of special effects wizardry that would put any rock concert to shame. The sound system is also set up and tested, as are all the lights. This is the difference between WCW and the minor leagues of professional wrestling. The magic environment created by the lights, music, and fireworks are like an assault on the senses of the viewer. It is all icing on the cake of the great action WCW provides.

When WCW holds a live event, it is incredible. Put that event on live television, and it becomes that much bigger. Multiple television cameras are set up, in addition to microphones to pick up every sound that occurs in the ring. To handle all of this, and to provide the best presentation possible to the fans watching at home, two large production trucks are set up at the arena. Inside, directors and editors work to take all the camera angles, all the interviews, and all the pretaped segments, and put them together into a cohesive package. From there, the show is beamed via satellite all over the world.

Booker T

Some wrestlers choose to go with a power attack, muscling around their rivals with brawn and size. Others use their speed to propel a high-flying attack on the opposition. Booker T is that rare breed that can mix both styles, tailoring his attack to exploit his opponents' weaknesses. This ability to adapt to any situation has made Booker T one of the most successful performers in WCW history, holding many WCW championships, including TV, tag team, and heavyweight titles—with more sure to come.

Hard Worker

When he first arrived in WCW with his brother, Stevie Ray, many figured Booker T would always remain in tag team competition. However, when Stevie Ray chose to become part of the nWo, Booker T was forced to enter the world of singles wrestling, a decision he's certainly never regretted. Booker T wants to be remembered for always doing the right thing and not for taking an easy path to success. His career thus far in WCW has shown that hard work truly does pay off.

Booker T

- Height: 6' 3"
- Weight: 250 lbs.
- Hometown: Harlem, NY
- Birthday: May 1
- Debut: 1989
- Finishing maneuver: Missile Dropkick/Harlem Hangover
- Titles held: WCW World Television Title, WCW World Tag Team Title, WCW World Heavyweight Title

Before their final breakup, Booker T and brother Stevie Ray broke all records as Harlem Heat. They held the WCW World Tag Team Title on 10 separate occasions, defeating brawlers, scientific grapplers, powerhouses, and high-flyers during their illustrious tag career. Should the two ever put their differences aside and re-form their combo, they could possibly go on to win another 10 tag titles!

Booker T has held the WCW World Television Title six times, a record that no one to date has even come close to matching. It's quite a compliment to be considered the greatest TV champ ever, especially when you look at some of the other legends who have held the belt. Most experts would agree though that Booker T is the finest wrestler to hold the honor.

When Booker T is on the defensive, he has a method of getting back on track that is exclusively his. He goes into a breakdancing backspin, which brings him to his feet to deliver a flying forearm or one of his devastating kicks. WCW announcer Mark Madden has referred to this move as the "spin-a-rooni," but whatever you call it, it sure is effective!

Blood Feud

The breakup of Harlem Heat and his deteriorating relationship with his brother still rankle with Booker T. When Stevie Ray wanted to join the nWo, and Booker T did not, many expected them to feud. For a while, brotherly love kept one from engaging the other, and they simply followed separate careers. But after a brief reconciliation, Stevie Ray viciously betrayed his own blood and started the one war that Booker T never wanted.

Spectacular Attack

Booker T's multifaceted attack has been known to take down opponents of all styles and sizes. What defense is there when a 6′ 3″ man swings his muscular legs into motion for an ax kick or Harlem Sidekick? Once an opponent is down, it's only a matter of time before Booker T scales the ropes and delivers the Missile Dropkick or Harlem Hangover (a spectacular flip off the top rope) and gets the pin.

Towering Talent

Booker T was once well-known for his red hot entrance, which included towering walls of flame and the classic Harlem Heat music. However, J. Biggs, at the urging of Stevie Ray, took legal action to prevent Booker T from using the music and flame entrance. They even forced him to stop wearing his trademark tights and took away the "T" from his ring name, giving it to Big T. One thing they could not take away though, was his talent. No matter how he is packaged, Booker is still an incredible competitor.

Big T

You would think that someone like Big T would want nothing to do with a shifty businessman like Mr. J. Biggs. After all, Big T prefers to settle matters with his fists, not through lawyers and contracts. But their mutual love and respect have brought them together. Love and respect for money that is! As long as J. Biggs can ensure Big T's bank account keeps getting bigger, this is one alliance that will stay strong.

Remember the old phrase "you wouldn't want to meet him in a dark alley?" Well, when it comes to Big T, you wouldn't want to meet him in broad daylight either! Seemingly never in a good mood, Big T leaves broken and battered bodies wherever he travels. It's almost as if he doesn't know his own strength, the way he bounces opponents around the ring, but the truth is, he knows exactly what he's doing. He enjoys making people suffer. A relative newcomer to WCW, Big T is street tough and gang tested, and, along with Stevie Ray, comprises the new Harlem Heat.

Harlem Heat

While Big T certainly loves getting the chance to brutalize new opposition, he is also motivated by the almighty dollar. It was the thought of making big money that led Big T to join with Mr. J. Biggs and Stevie Ray to take the form Harlem Heat, Inc. The fact that he would be doing it at the expense of Booker was just icing on the cake. With that first big check came the desire for more, and now it is probably just a matter of time before the new Harlem Heat follows in the footsteps of the former, and goes after the WCW World Tag Team Title. After all, nothing will bring Big T more money than receiving a champion's salary. Plus, it will guarantee new challengers for him to beat up!

The original Harlem Heat were two brothers, Stevie Ray and Booker T, so it was only natural that they gelled in the ring. However, it is truly amazing to see the teamwork of the new Harlem Heat in action. Some experts are already predicting greatness for this version of the Heat.

Big T

- Height: 6' 4"
- Weight: 300 lbs.
- Hometown: Pearl River, MS
- Birthday: June 6
- Debut: 1989
- Finishing maneuver: Tiger Driver
- Phrase: "I'm the only 'T' in WCW!"

STEVIE RAY

Can you feel the Heat? Well if you can, you better realize that it is owned by Stevie Ray. This grappler is so possessive of the Harlem Heat reputation that he created a corporation, Harlem Heat, Inc., and has made sure that its trademark tights, music, entrance, and name are all owned by him. He even won the rights to the "T" in his former partner Booker T's name. Although, with the brothers currently at odds, Stevie now has the power to keep Booker T from using those things that he was previously identified with, the brothers' disagreements will never detract from what a great team Harlem Heat was.

The new Harlem Heat bears little resemblance to the original team. Sure, the music, tights, and entrance are all the same, but the style has changed. Big T is a full-blown powerhouse, not an aerial artist like Booker T. Together, Big T and Stevie Ray present quite a different form of attack—one which relies heavily on the use of power moves. Their double team Tiger Driver has already stacked up plenty of wins for the team, and some say it is only a matter of time until they begin their first WCW World Tag Team Title reign.

THE NEW HEAT

There is much more to Stevie Ray than just his relationship with his brother. He has shown that he is a very capable singles competitor and now, with partner Big T, once again looks to dominate the tag team scene in WCW. Will the new Harlem Heat be able to win championship gold and escape the shadow that comes with using the Harlem Heat name? Or is this just another transitional period for Stevie Ray, like his time as a member of the New World Order? We'll just have to wait and see, but one thing can be assured. Whatever Stevie Ray plans to accomplish in WCW, he'll always have the Heat.

Stevie Ray has always been proud of the way he was brought up on the streets of Harlem. He's also proud of the way he used those street smarts to get where he is today. He frequently returns to his old neighborhood and sometimes brings back a few friends with him, such as Big T and Cassius. Stevie Ray has worked his way up from nothing, without forgetting where he came from. He still exhibits the same hunger he had on the streets, only now he uses it to create success in the ring.

STEVIE RAY
- **Height: 6' 5"**
- **Weight: 265 lbs.**
- **Hometown: Harlem, NY**
- **Birthday: August 22**
- **Debut: 1989**
- **Finishing maneuver: Slap Jack**
- **Phrase: "I'm the real Harlem Heat"**
- **Titles held: WCW World Tag Team Title**

Tag Teams

Originally invented in Australia, tag team wrestling is now a staple of every WCW event held around the world. The basic premise is that one man from each team is in the ring grappling, while his partner stands in a corner of the ring, waiting to be tagged in. Once tagged, the previous combatant has five seconds to leave the ring. Of course, it is how a tag team uses that five second window when they can both be in the ring simultaneously that determines how effective the team will be.

DISCO INFERNO

He demands to be taken seriously as an athlete, but how can you take seriously anyone who calls himself the Disco Inferno? While his name may sound comic and dated, Disco is one wrestler you should indeed take seriously. A two-time former WCW World Television Champion, he has proven time and time again that when he's focused, he can beat any wrestler on any night. He's definitely become a scholar of the game, although he's chosen some rather unorthodox methods to improve his skills. At one point in his career, Disco claimed to have a new finishing hold that was practically inescapable. Unfortunately, it was also hard to remember, and Disco actually had to carry a piece of paper with a diagram drawn on it to remind him of the proper way to apply it!

Disco prides himself on his superior dancing skills, but he hasn't found too many fans of his boogying gyrations. He once became embroiled in a feud with former tag team partner Alex Wright (now called Berlyn) over who had the best moves on the dance floor. Had they concentrated as much on their teamwork, they'd have been WCW World Tag Team Champions! As far as the fans were concerned, neither of these dancing fools had any rhythm!

CRUISERWEIGHT

Determined to get a shot at the cruiserweight title, Disco began to diet and exercise constantly, sometimes right up until bell time. On the occasions that he did bring his weight down low enough to compete, he was usually too exhausted and quickly lost his matches!

While Disco wears some truly outrageous outfits these days, his initial ring attire looked like it came right out of the '70s! He used to wear polyester bellbottom pants with matching vest and black silk shirt. As if that wasn't enough, he also wore tights with "Shake Your Booty" across his rear!

DISCO INFERNO

- Height: 6'
- Weight: 238 lbs.
- Hometown: Brooklyn, NY
- Birthday: November 12
- Debut: November 20, 1991
- Finishing maneuver: The Last Dance
- Phrase: "Hey, Paisan!"
- Titles held: WCW World Television Title, WCW Cruiserweight Title

DEBT COLLECTORS

When the Mamalukes first came into WCW, they had one thing on their minds: roughing up Disco Inferno for the money he owed Mr. Marinara. Somehow Disco ended up managing them and took them all the way to the WCW World Tag Team Championship! Now, Disco proclaims himself to be the "Manager of Champions."

THE MAMALUKES

A huge, muscular man with incredible athletic ability, Johnny made a rather unusual debut when he joined in the thick of tag team competition—as a debt collector! The perfect compliment to his veteran partner Big Vito, Johnny adds youth and an incredible arsenal of maneuvers to the tandem. The Mamalukes are an impressive combo and have already become WCW World Tag Team Champions. Of course, don't ever let them hear you call them Mamalukes. If they address you, and you're not stunned speechless by fear, make sure to call them the Paisans!

THE SILENT ONE

If you were to say that Johnny is a man of few words, you'd be overstating it. Johnny rarely speaks, and when he does it's usually to Vito or Disco. He shies away from interviews, instead allowing the other Mamalukes to speak on behalf of the team. Where he does most of the talking is in the ring, and the words he uses are the punches and kicks he repeatedly lays into his opponent. And they never ask him to repeat himself!

DISCO AND THE MAMALUKES

The relationship between Disco Inferno and Big Vito has been interesting, to say the least. Originally, Vito was to collect money from Disco, and when the WCW star couldn't produce, Vito was going to make him "sleep with the fishes." However, Disco somehow got on Vito's good side and became his manager, leading him and Johnny to the WCW World Tag Team Championship!

Big Vito certainly holds his family close to his heart, and sometimes it gets the better of him. When his sister got married, it was arranged for the reception to be held backstage during a *Nitro* event, so Vito could attend. Unfortunately, David Flair, Crowbar, and Daffney attended as well, uninvited. The ensuing food fight embarrassed and enraged Vito, who vowed revenge.

MAMALUKES

- **Height: Johnny 6' 3"; Vito 6' 2"**
- **Weight: Johnny 255 lbs.; Vito 250 lbs.**
- **Debut: 1999**
- **Hometown: Johnny, New York City; Vito, Staten Island, NY**
- **Finishing maneuver: Johnny, Elbow Drop; Vito, Implant DDT**
- **Phrase: Johnny, "You want to sleep with the fishes?"; Vito, "It's Paisans, not Mamalukes!"**
- **Titles held: WCW World Tag Team Title**

Big Poppa Pump

Over the course of their partnership, Rick and Scott Steiner have won over a dozen tag team titles and have certainly shown their dominance in that division. Ironically, in their early days together, Scott was seen as the quiet sideman to the wacky Rick. Many words can be used to describe Big Poppa Pump today, but quiet certainly isn't one of them!

Perhaps the greatest physical specimen in the history of wrestling, the man the ladies call the "Big Bad Booty Daddy" is also one of the greatest wrestlers in WCW. A pivotal part of the New World Order, Scott Steiner is one man that no one wants to mess with. He has innovated dozens of new maneuvers and has racked up titles and victories with ease over the years. His legendary tag team with brother Rick is considered by many to be the best team that ever existed. They have even performed on a regular basis for crowds of over 50,000 people in Japan.

The Frankensteiner

Although he is more known for his feats of strength now, Scott invented one of the most emulated maneuvers in the world, the Frankensteiner. A modified version of the Mexican huracanrana, Big Poppa Pump changed it slightly to be done from a standing position, rather than from the air. Occasionally, he will pull it out of his arsenal, usually flipping his rival from the top rope.

Scott Steiner has made quite a mark, not only in the ring, but in deceiving people as well. He tricked his brother Rick several times into thinking that he had left the nWo. He assisted Buff Bagwell in deceiving the world after Buff's neck injury. However, his greatest deception was in convincing the fans that he was retiring after a back injury, only to fool everyone and rejoin the nWo.

Big Poppa Pump

- Height: 6' 1"
- Weight: 235 lbs.
- Hometown: Detroit, MI
- Birthday: July 29
- Debut: 1986
- Finishing maneuver: Steiner Recliner
- Phrase: "Big Poppa Pump is your hookup, holler if you hear me!"
- Titles held: WCW World Tag Team Title, WCW United States Title, WCW United States Tag Team Title, WCW World Television Title

Big in Japan

The land of the rising sun has been a favorite stomping ground for Scott for several years. He and brother Rick won numerous titles in Japan and spent almost two years competing exclusively for New Japan Pro-Wrestling, headlining shows at the huge Tokyo Dome, an enormous baseball stadium that the Steiners regularly sold out!

Since joining the nWo, Big Poppa Pump has concentrated on singles gold, and he's been successful, winning both the WCW World Television Title and WCW United States Title. The real prize, the WCW World Heavyweight Title has still eluded him, but with a long career ahead, it is only a matter of time before Big Poppa has the big belt!

Joining the nWo

How attractive is the power of the New World Order? Well, Scott wanted to be a member so badly, that on February 22, 1998, he not only gave up the WCW World Tag Team Title, he turned on his own brother, joining forces with Scott Hall and Kevin Nash. While members have come and gone, Steiner has remained committed to the nWo.

The Man who has it All?

What is truly scary is that Steiner has accomplished all of his achievements at such a young age. He has many years to go before he calls it a day on his career and seems destined to go down in history as one of the best wrestlers ever. Of course, almost as important to Steiner as his wrestling legacy is his reputation with the fairer sex—Big Poppa Pump is always known to have two or three beautiful ladies locked onto his muscular arms! So, combine an incredible physique, an arsenal of unique moves, a killer instinct, and a bevy of beauties, and you have Big Poppa Pump, Scott Steiner.

NITRO

The landscape of professional wrestling changed forever when WCW launched *Nitro*, a program that has become the company's TV flagship. Broadcast live every Monday night from sold-out arenas across the country, *Nitro* is two hours of nonstop action and excitement where anything can happen. Well-known names reinvent themselves with new identities, stars are born, and feuds start, escalate, and are settled—all during episodes of *Nitro*. Not a week passes without some surprises. The show has become so eventful that it's now the one program wrestling fans can't afford to miss.

BUFF BAGWELL

He is probably the best wrestler in WCW to never hold a singles title. Buff Bagwell has it all—his tremendous physique and power are complemented by his speed and agility. Although he has the face of a model, he isn't afraid to tear it up in an all-out brawl. Hugely confident in his abilities, his massive ego actually helps him in the ring, since he refuses to allow himself to be beaten. Second to none, in his eyes at least, Bagwell wants it all, and he wants it now.

In 1990, Buff was voted WCW Rookie of the Year. A great deal was expected of him, which may have held him back, as he was placed in matches with far more experienced grapplers.

BUFF BLOCKBUSTER

Bagwell's finishing maneuver is The Buff Blockbuster—one of the most effective moves in WCW. After stunning his opponent, Bagwell leaps to the second rope and measures up his enemy. In one deft motion, he leaps over him, flips forward, and grabs him by the back of the head. His adversary slams right into the mat, and Buff scores another victory.

BUFF BAGWELL
- Height: 6' 1"
- Weight: 240 lbs.
- Hometown: Marietta, GA
- Birthday: January 10th
- Debut: 1990
- Finishing maneuver: The Buff Blockbuster
- Phrase: "I'm Buff, and I'm the stuff"
- Titles held: WCW World Tag Team Title

Just how much do the ladies love Buff's stuff? Maybe less than we think! When Billy Kidman's KidCam was stolen, the thief filmed Buff putting his moves on the WCW ladies. Daffney, Miss Hancock, Symphony, and Elizabeth all turned him down flat! Stories that Buff was involved with Kimberly, the wife of Diamond Dallas Page, turned out to be untrue as well.

Tag Team

Buff Bagwell is one of greatest tag team wrestlers in WCW history. He has held the WCW World Tag Team Title on several occasions, and with more than one partner. Defeating teams like Harlem Heat and the Nasty Boys, Bagwell showed that he can gel with any partner of any style. With an amazing record of tag team gold successes, Bagwell now has set his sights set on individual glory.

Buff Bagwell was one of the most solid members of the New World Order. But a day finally came when Bagwell could no longer put up with the egomania of Hulk Hogan and Scott Steiner (considering Bagwell's high opinion of himself, that's not surprising). Maybe it's just a coincidence that the nWo began to crumble around the time that Buff left. Then again, maybe it's not.

Mr. Popular

Bagwell's popularity, particularly among female fans, is extraordinary. His face adorns posters and T-shirts, and it seems the merchandise department just can't keep up with the demand for Buff's stuff! Buff has even translated his success in the ring into a movie career, starring in *The Day of The Warrior* and *Return to Savage Beach.* Buff has a humorous side, too, and his impressions of Curt Hennig, Scott Steiner, and Ernest Miller have made fans roar with laughter, while the subjects seethed with rage. No one man is the perfect wrestler, but Buff Bagwell is certainly as close as you will come.

We aren't quite clear what Buff Bagwell refers to when he says he is the "stuff," but if he means natural athletic ability and movie star charisma, then we fully agree.

TRO
UNIVERSITY OF NORTH

Rick Steiner

He's the big brother of Big Poppa Pump, but that is the least of the things Rick Steiner is known for. An outstanding amateur wrestler at Michigan State, perhaps no other collegiate wrestler has made such an easy transition to the pro ranks. Complimenting his amazing array of suplexes with an equally impressive clothesline and top rope Bulldog, this barking master of the ring is always a force to be reckoned with. Did we say barking? We certainly did, as the "Dog-Faced Gremlin" (DFG) has been known to act like a pit bull in the ring, staking his territory and attacking any intruders to his ring.

Early in his career, a young Rick Steiner allowed himself to be a part of the Varsity Club, a ruthless rule-breaking group of former collegiate wrestlers, whose ranks included Mike Rotunda and Kevin Sullivan. They were successful in the late '80s, before going their separate ways. A full decade later, they reunited, and have been causing havoc in WCW ever since. Who says you can't go back to school?

Steiner has become known for some strange behavior in the past, such as talking to a face drawn on his hand (he called it Alex). More recently, he has told loyal fans that the DFG was now going to do things in his own manner, which included turning on longtime friend Sting. In his own words, "if you don't like me, bite me."

Rick Steiner
- Height: 5' 11"
- Weight: 248 lbs.
- Hometown: Detroit, MI
- Birthday: March 9
- Debut: 1983
- Finishing maneuver: Top rope Bulldog
- Phrase: "Welcome to the dog pound!"
- Titles held: WCW United States Tag Team Title, WCW World Tag Team Title, WCW World Television Title.

Fresh Fighter

While Steiner has had singles success in the television division, ironically his greatest success came against a tag team. When his scheduled partner, Buff Bagwell, walked out on him during a tag team title match against Scott Steiner and The Giant, Rick opted to go it alone. Incredibly, he defeated them both to win the title, then went on to defeat Scott again that same night in a no-disqualification match. As a final jab at the New World Order, Steiner selected as his new partner the next night Judy Bagwell, Buff's mom!

Brothers in arms

The Steiner brothers are neck and neck with the original Harlem Heat in the race for title of "greatest brother tag team ever" with Harlem Heat having more WCW tag championships, and the Steiners holding far more titles in the wrestling mecca of Japan. These two teams have met on countless occasions, and although a rematch anytime soon seems unlikely, every wrestling fan's dream is to someday see the two sides re-form and do battle again.

Long before Rick became one half of the Steiner brothers tag team, he carved out quite a career on his own. He held the WCW United States Tag Team Title with the late Eddie Gilbert, and also won the WCW World Television Title by defeating his former Varsity Club teammate Mike Rotunda. When the brothers later broke up, Steiner again found success in the WCW World Television division and even won the WCW World Tag Team Title by himself!

nWo

No one is quite sure to this day what prompted Rick Steiner to turn his back on Sting and WCW to join the nWo. After all, he had been one of the most loyal wrestlers WCW had had in its war with the rebel group of wrestlers. Perhaps he just wanted to team with his brother again. Whatever the reason, Steiner certainly didn't stay with the nWo, and soon he was relying on the one person he always knew he could trust—himself.

The moves

How powerful is Rick Steiner? Well, his clotheslines are so devastating that they are referred to as "Steinerlines." If that isn't impressive enough, Steiner has shown that he can suplex anyone of any size, and from nearly any position in the ring. When Steiner mixes that incredible power with the added momentum of leaping off the top rope for his patented Bulldog, no one gets up.

NITRO GIRLS

Football and basketball can have all the cheerleaders they want, but they'll never measure up to WCW's very own group of dancers—the Nitro Girls. This incredible dance ensemble performs in front of WCW fans at *Nitro* and *Thunder* events every single week. Since they were formed by Kimberly, the Nitro Girls have gone through a few lineup changes, as different dancers have come and gone. However, this has not affected their popularity, and their swimsuit calendar is a sure sellout at merchandise stands whenever WCW rolls into town.

The Artist

One of the more unusual stories in WCW history is that of The Artist. After an incredible run of successes early in his career under the name Prince Iaukea, this Polynesian superstar underwent a bizarre personality change. Now regarding himself as a successful recording artist (although nothing resembling music comes out of him), The Artist discarded the native dress he formerly wore, and instead opted for a flamboyant, decidedly purple, wardrobe. He also refused to be referred to by his former name, instead demanding to be called "The Artist Formerly Known As Prince Iaukea," or simply, "The Artist."

Almost as much of a mystery as The Artist is his valet, Paisley. She does most of the talking for him and often seems to be the boss. Yet, after every match, he motions for her to crawl on her hands and knees to him!

Flying DDT

While it may not be as flamboyant as his entrance lights and wardrobe, The Artist's finishing maneuver is nevertheless one of the most devastating in the business today. Rather than just using a standard DDT, The Artist instead stands on the second rope, then leaps off and grabs his opponent by the head on the way down. His adversary's head slams into the mat with brutal force, and from there on The Artist's victory is assured.

When he was just plain Prince Iaukea, The Artist had one of the most incredible rookie years in the history of the business. He won the WCW World Television Title from rugged veteran Steven Regal just months before he celebrated his first year in wrestling. He continued his hot streak, even scoring a pinfall win over Rey Mysterio Jr.

The Artist Formerly Known As Prince Iaukea

- Height: 5' 11"
- Weight: 219 lbs.
- Hometown: Honolulu, HI
- Debut: April 1996
- Finishing maneuver: Leaping DDT
- Accompanied by: Paisley
- Titles held: WCW World Television Title, WCW Cruiserweight Title

Against Lash Leroux

When you think of the cruiserweight division of WCW, you think of high-flying, head-on wrestling, going by at a blindingly fast pace. You usually wouldn't associate the division with the type of psychological warfare that The Artist engages in. Yet he was successful in defeating Lash LeRoux and winning the WCW World Cruiserweight Title in a tournament final, so now these pure wrestlers better learn to deal with The Artist's distracting appearance and entrance, if they have any hopes of defeating him.

Cpl. Cajun

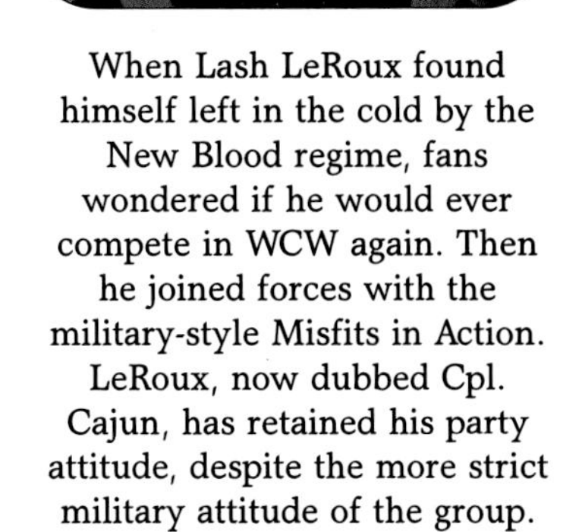

When Lash LeRoux found himself left in the cold by the New Blood regime, fans wondered if he would ever compete in WCW again. Then he joined forces with the military-style Misfits in Action. LeRoux, now dubbed Cpl. Cajun, has retained his party attitude, despite the more strict military attitude of the group.

Were you there when a young Michael Jordan first stepped onto the basketball court? How about the first time Aerosmith ever performed on stage? Well, the feeling you would have had then is the same feeling you get from watching Lash LeRoux now. You are seeing the earliest days of an inevitable legend. It seems hard to grasp, but in 15, 20, 25, or more years from now, people will look at Lash LeRoux and see the standard bearer for the sport. Like Sting in the late '80s, Lash is a breakout performer just waiting to show the world what he's got.

Bourbon Street Blues

Lash certainly knows how to mix flash and substance into an effective style. His Bourbon Street Blues combo sees him land a series of jabs, drop down into a split, then pop back up and rock his opponent with a vicious lariat. Lash's quickness and speed make it an excellent prelude to his Whiplash finisher, or allow him to take back the advantage when his opponent tries to dictate the pace of the bout.

The Whiplash

The key to being effective in the ring is knowing how to be able to end a match, and Lash LeRoux has an incredible match ending maneuver in the Whiplash. After lifting his opponent into a fireman's carry, LeRoux throws off the guy's legs and brings him down in front of him, landing him on his neck and shoulders. The opponent is now stunned and in the perfect pinning position. Rarely does the poor guy kick out from such a prone and abject state!

Cpl. Cajun

- **Height: 5' 11"**
- **Weight: 221 lbs.**
- **Hometown: New Orleans, LA**
- **Birthday: November 22**
- **Debut: July 1998**
- **Finishing maneuver: The Whiplash**

MEET

Training

Football players play once a week for a few months. Baseball players spend half of the game sitting on the bench. Boxers fight a dozen times a year, maybe. Only in professional wrestling do the athletes perform, almost night after night, for 365 days a year. There is no off season in professional wrestling. That is why the superstars of WCW are among the finest athletes in the world today. It takes a special drive and determination to attain these heights. Hundreds of men and women each year strive to become part of WCW, but only a small fraction get to step through the ropes. When a wrestler thinks he's ready to join the best in the world, he enters the Power Plant, WCW's training facility, where the serious competitor is separated from the pretender.

Being muscular can certainly look impressive, but without proper cardiovascular training, those musclemen will be sucking air after five minutes with the likes of Kidman, Rey Mysterio Jr., or Juventud Guerrera. That's because these wrestlers constantly make sure they are in a superb state of fitness in order to compete at their top pace—and not lose their wind while doing so. Aerobics and calisthenics are the keys to making sure your heart and lungs are ready for the rigors of the ring wars.

Some wrestlers practice their high-flying moves from the diving board of a swimming pool, with the safety of hitting only water if it goes wrong. Ultimately though, there's no better training than getting in the ring and applying your trade. The ring is the first thing set up at WCW events, to allow wrestlers time to work on their holds and moves, as well as get the opportunity to familiarize themselves with the ropes and mat, which may vary slightly in looseness or tightness. Some wrestlers have gone as far as having their own rings built, so they can work on moves at home. At least they don't have to worry about outside interference!

The final aspect, and perhaps the most important, is strategy. No matter how fit your body is, and how many spectacular moves you can perform, if you don't go into your match with a game plan, you'll be staring up at the ring lights when the referee counts to three. A good strategy is one that capitalizes on your strengths, while taking advantage of your opponent's weaknesses. Simply, the rule is always study your opponent. Get to know his style and techniques from previous matches.

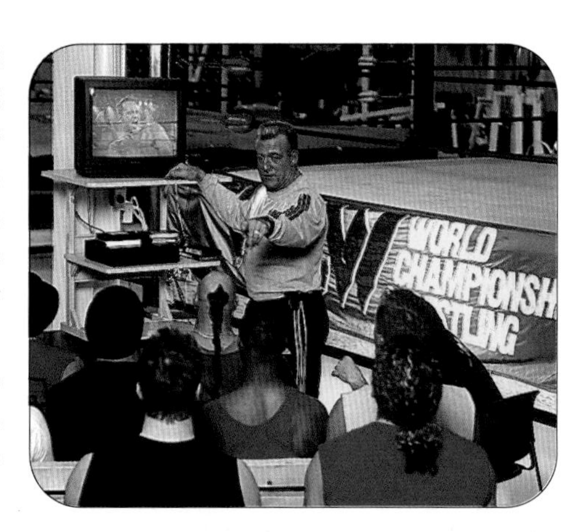

HARDCORE

Wrestlers who make it to the upper echelons of WCW are among the finest trained athletes in the world. But that doesn't mean they won't get hardcore on occasion. Hardcore matches, where falls count anywhere in the building—not just in the ring—and all weapons are legal, have become very popular, not only with the fans, but with certain brawlers in the WCW locker room who see hardcore as the perfect opportunity to show how tough they are. Matches have gone all over the place, sometimes even outside the arena, and everything from trashcans to fire extinguishers has been used to annihilate the opposition!

SURGE

BAM BAM BIGELOW

At an imposing 6′ 3″ and close to 400 pounds, Bam Bam Bigelow is already an awesome competitor. Throw in the fact that this tattooed monster also has uncanny speed and agility, and you can easily see why he would be feared by potential opponents. However, we've only scratched the surface, as this hardcore madman has no fear of pain, and gladly brings a garbage can of weapons into the ring—despite knowing that he'll probably end up on the receiving end of some of them! Of course, that's a small price to pay to get in some shots of his own!

From a distance, you might think Bam Bam has hair. Get up close, and you will see that his huge dome is actually covered with a tattoo of a fireball! His arms are also tattooed, but it's his head of fire that you'll notice first!

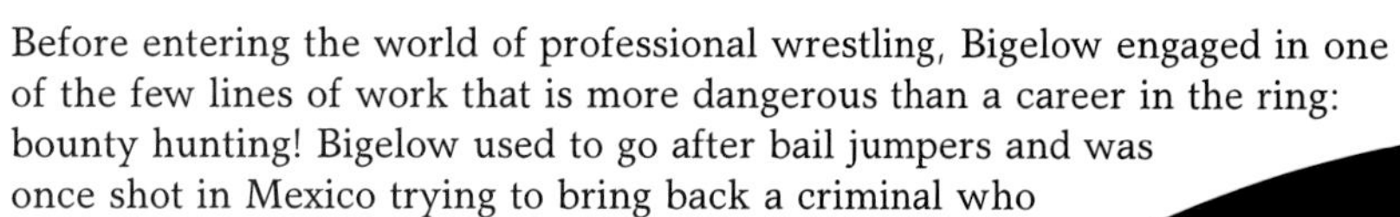

Before entering the world of professional wrestling, Bigelow engaged in one of the few lines of work that is more dangerous than a career in the ring: bounty hunting! Bigelow used to go after bail jumpers and was once shot in Mexico trying to bring back a criminal who was attempting to flee the country rather than face trial. That tends to make a superplex through a table seem easy by comparison!

GARBAGE DISPOSAL

Bam Bam could easily be regarded as one of the most complete wrestlers in the business, mixing mat skills, high flying, and power moves in the ring. However, he is truly at home brawling through a crowd, slamming his adversary with garbage cans and smashing them through tables. Although he did enjoy a brief alliance with Diamond Dallas Page and Chris Kanyon in the Triad, he prefers to go it alone, answering to no one but himself. He has also shown no fear in challenging some of the toughest men on the planet, probably because he realizes that few, if any, are truly tougher than he is.

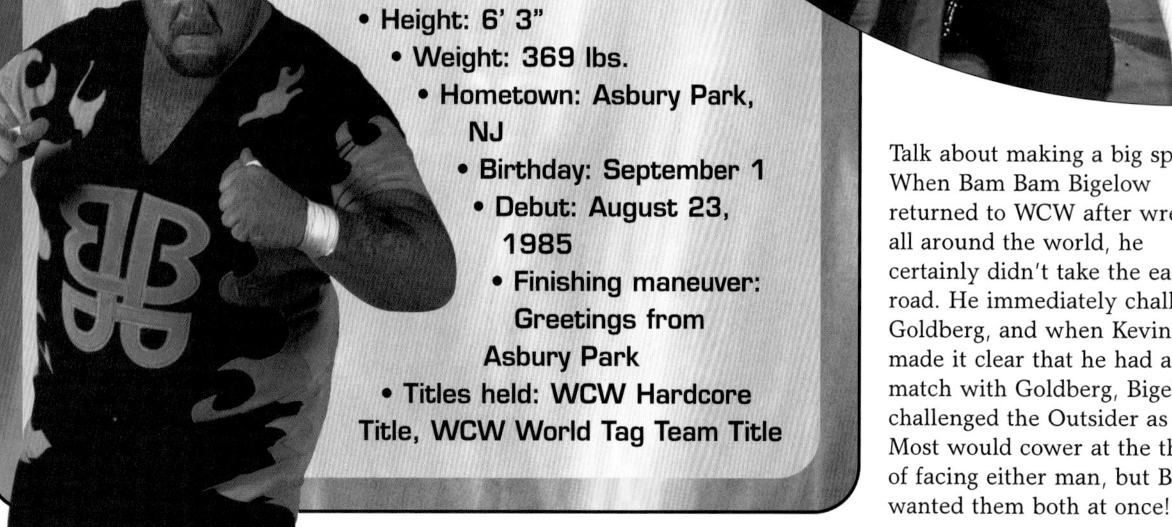

BAM BAM BIGELOW

- Height: 6′ 3″
- Weight: 369 lbs.
- Hometown: Asbury Park, NJ
- Birthday: September 1
- Debut: August 23, 1985
- Finishing maneuver: Greetings from Asbury Park
- Titles held: WCW Hardcore Title, WCW World Tag Team Title

Talk about making a big splash! When Bam Bam Bigelow returned to WCW after wrestling all around the world, he certainly didn't take the easy road. He immediately challenged Goldberg, and when Kevin Nash made it clear that he had a match with Goldberg, Bigelow challenged the Outsider as well! Most would cower at the thought of facing either man, but Bigelow wanted them both at once!

JUMPING MONSTER

With his immense size and power, Bigelow's finishing move—"Greetings from Asbury Park"—seems like a natural, as he lifts opponents over his shoulder before driving them down headfirst onto the mat. However, this 369-pounder can also scale the top rope and fly off with a devastating head butt as well. His agility for a big man impressed Japanese fans so much that they dubbed him "The Jumping Monster."

The New Jersey Triad of Bigelow, Diamond Dallas Page, and Chris Kanyon certainly pulled a fast one when they won the WCW World Tag Team Title. Kanyon was working as a substitute partner with Perry Saturn, when he turned on Saturn, allowing Page and Bigelow to win the gold. After the match, Kanyon joined them to form the Triad, and any two of the three members were allowed to defend the titles.

BORN FIGHTER

When Bigelow was first starting to train as a wrestler, he received quite a bit of attention. Before he even fought his first professional match, he was featured in *Sports Illustrated* and on *Entertainment Tonight*. When he finally did make his debut, it was at the legendary New York nightclub, *Studio 54*, where he defeated three opponents.

BRIAN KNOBS

They certainly don't come any nastier than Brian Knobs, one of the innovators of hardcore wrestling in WCW. Marching to the beat of his own drum, Knobs has earned success in WCW just by being himself and by applying the same attitude to the ring that he has to his daily life. He takes whatever he wants, and if you want to stop him, you have to fight him. This veteran has been through it all, and loved every minute of it.

It is the most disgusting maneuver in the history of professional wrestling. It's never actually won a match, but only serves to embarrass opponents. It's the Pit Stop, whereby Knobs grabs his opponent by the back of the head, raises his other arm, and crams the poor guy's face into his sweaty, smelly armpit.

HARDCORE
To date, Knobs is the only man to hold the WCW Hardcore Title twice. He defeated the popular Norman Smiley for the belt, but lost it to Bam Bam Bigelow. He regained it with help from Fit Finlay, before losing it again to the unlikely combo of 3 Count.

BRIAN KNOBS
- Height: 6' 1"
- Weight: 295 lbs.
- Hometown: Allentown, PA
- Birthday: May 6
- Debut: 1985
- Finishing maneuver: Pit Stop
- Phrase: "It's time to get nastisized!"
- Titles held: WCW Hardcore Title, WCW World Tag Team Title

FIT FINLAY

There are few tougher than Fit Finlay. The man known as the "Belfast Bruiser" has made a worldwide reputation as a take-no-prisoners wrestler, mixing stiff matwork with hard-nosed barroom brawling. Finlay reminds some of the lone man at the back of a bar, keeping quiet until someone rubs him the wrong way. After that, Finlay disposes of the problem, and takes pride and pleasure in doing so. Then he goes back to what he was doing.

Of course, when no problem presents itself, Finlay just goes out and creates one for himself. He's made more than his fair share of trouble in WCW and is constantly looking for another fight. Although he is a former WCW World Television Champion, titles mean little to this man. The feel of a gold belt is nothing to Finlay compared to the feel of an opponent's bones breaking in his hands!

HARDCORE
Before WCW ever had a championship for the style, Finlay never shied away from fighting hardcore and using weapons in his matches. Ironically, while he was one of many who claimed to be the "hardcore champion" before the belt was created, he has yet to capture the gold and make it official. While Finlay doesn't need the belt to validate his toughness, there is little doubt that the strap will one day be his.

FIT FINLAY
- Height: 5' 10"
- Weight: 230 lbs.
- Hometown: Belfast, Northern Ireland
- Debut: 1978
- Finishing maneuver: Tombstone Piledriver
- Titles held: WCW World Television Title

NORMAN SMILEY

He is one of the more unusual individuals in the WCW locker room and, at the same time, one of the most wildly popular. Norman Smiley spent almost 15 years building a reputation as a serious ring competitor, a master of mat technique. Then, one evening, while celebrating a successful maneuver, Norman started to dance in the ring. The "Big Wiggle" was born, and the English have finally repaid us for sending them the Twist back in the '60s. The Big Wiggle is loved by fans and loathed by opponents who witness it during matches.

When Norman was looking for ways to protect himself in hardcore matches, he found that donning sportswear was a good idea. Football pads or a baseball catcher's chest protector provided good impact resistance to body blows, and a helmet made a good weapon. Soon he was wearing the colors of the local sports team in each city, so Norman is always the hometown favorite!

It's incredible that the same straight-laced man who represented Britain in the 1990 Pat O'Connor Memorial Invitational Tag Team Tournament is now one of the most entertaining players to set foot in the ring. Opponents usually fail to take him seriously and find themselves tapping out to the "Norman Conquest!"

SMILIN' AND SCREAMIN'

"Screamin' Norman" has been known to howl in pain whenever he gets hit, particularly during hardcore matches. Occasionally, in fear of his opponents, Norman chooses to run and hide, screaming his head off, rather than face the challenge. Of course, once he gets down to business, he often emerges victorious, but until he gets over that initial fright, he'll scream like a banshee!

NORMAN SMILEY

- Height: 6' 2"
- Weight: 240 lbs.
- Hometown: London, England
- Debut: 1985
- Finishing maneuver: The Big Wiggle
- Phrase: "It's Wiggle Time!"
- Titles held: WCW Hardcore Title

Steel Cage

It is the most dangerous match in professional wrestling. When a dispute cannot be settled by any other means, the fighters are put in a steel cage. The ring is surrounded by 15-foot-high walls of chainlink fence and is sometimes roofed over so that no one can get in... or out. This cage not only becomes a barrier, but a weapon as well, with wrestlers being raked across the fencing, or rammed into its steel links. Steel Cage matches are not held very often, which shows just how dangerous they can be!

KEVIN NASH

A three-time WCW World Heavyweight Champion, a four-time WCW World Tag Team Champion, the commissioner of WCW, and he would like nothing better than to destroy the whole company?! Sounds unbelievable, but it's true. Kevin Nash has turned WCW upside down since the formation of the New World Order. What possible reason could such a talented wrestler have for wanting to make a fool of the top wrestling company in the world? Perhaps the answer lies in his past, when Kevin was a young wrestler forced to play ridiculous characters like Oz and Vinnie Vegas, by promoters who had no idea how to handle his talent.

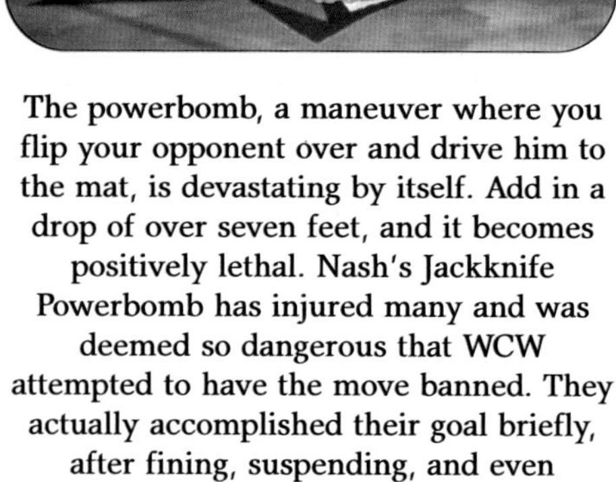

The powerbomb, a maneuver where you flip your opponent over and drive him to the mat, is devastating by itself. Add in a drop of over seven feet, and it becomes positively lethal. Nash's Jackknife Powerbomb has injured many and was deemed so dangerous that WCW attempted to have the move banned. They actually accomplished their goal briefly, after fining, suspending, and even arresting Nash for using the move to hurt his opponents unnecessarily.

POWER ABUSE

Some men were born to be great leaders. Others were born to abuse power. Kevin Nash, for better or worse, seems to be both of these. As leader of the nWo he ran roughshod over the company, but he has also managed to win a position of power within WCW on two separate occasions. As WCW commissioner, he stripped Sid Vicious of the WCW World Heavyweight Title, only to award it to himself!

KEVIN NASH

- **Height: 7' 1"**
- **Weight: 370 lbs.**
- **Hometown: Detroit, MI**
- **Birthday: July 9**
- **Debut: 1990**
- **Finishing maneuver: Jackknife Powerbomb**
- **Phrase: "Too sweet!"**
- **Titles held: WCW World Heavyweight Title, WCW World Tag Team Title**

You have to wonder what Kevin Nash really thinks of championships. Does he care about holding titles, or does he just enjoy taking them away from others? Shortly after winning the WCW World Title, he literally lay down and let Hulk Hogan pin him for it. Later, when Hogan was hoping he'd do it again, Nash refused. It seems Big Sexy just likes to laugh in the face of authority and do things his way!

Goldberg

It will someday be the answer to a wrestling trivia question. Who ended Goldberg's undefeated streak? Well, it was "Big Sexy" Kevin Nash who pinned Goldberg at *Starrcade '98* to win the WCW World Heavyweight Title. Of course, Nash couldn't do it on his own and needed the help of his long-time friend Scott Hall. During a chaotic moment in the bout, Hall, dressed as a security guard, stunned Goldberg with a police stun gun, rendering him unconscious and allowing Nash to score the historic (although tainted) pinfall.

Tag Team Greats

Could the Outsiders be the greatest tag team in WCW history? Having defeated the Steiner brothers, Harlem Heat, and even the dream team of Bret Hart and Bill Goldberg, it's hard to argue with the success that Kevin Nash and Scott Hall have had in the ring. Although the two have had periods of discontent between them, when the four-time WCW World Tag Team Champions are on the same page, they are virtually unstoppable.

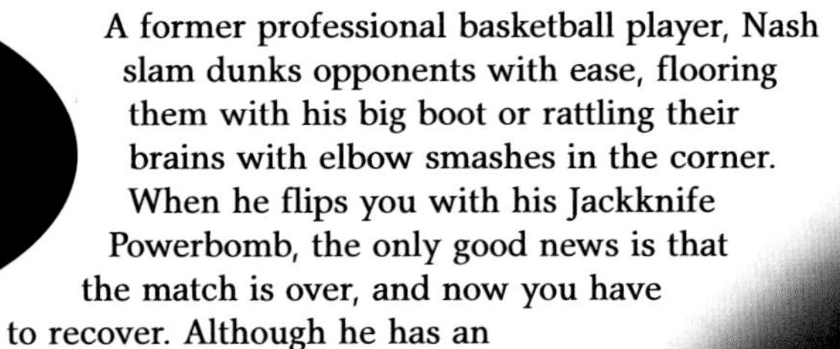

A former professional basketball player, Nash slam dunks opponents with ease, flooring them with his big boot or rattling their brains with elbow smashes in the corner. When he flips you with his Jackknife Powerbomb, the only good news is that the match is over, and now you have to recover. Although he has an incredible sense of humor, he also has a vicious streak, and it's hard to tell from day to day if Nash wants to play stand-up or executioner. One of the truly elite superstars in WCW, it will be some time before anyone can stop him doing whatever he wants, whenever he wants.

Chaos Outside

June 10, 1996 will be a date long remembered by WCW fans. That's the day Kevin Nash joined his best friend Scott Hall on a live broadcast of *WCW Nitro*. One week later, Nash made his presence felt by powerbombing the then WCW senior vice president, Eric Bischoff, through an interview stage. The chaos the Outsiders brought to WCW could be summed up in the simple phrase that became their calling card: "We're taking over!"

Scott Hall

He's one of the most controversial figures in wrestling and the catalyst that changed the industry forever. Scott Hall was the first piece of the puzzle that would become known as the New World Order. Always walking to the ring with the confidence befitting a superstar of his magnitude, Hall is considered to be one of the finest athletes in the history of the sport, a five-time WCW World Tag Team Champion, two-time WCW United States Champion, and a former WCW World Television Champion as well. He loves the gold around his waist almost as much as he loves defeating opponent and after opponent.

"How many of you came here tonight to see WCW?" is the first part of the survey Scott Hall likes to take before his matches. "Now, how many of you came to see the nWo?" is the second part. Regardless of whether fans chant for the New World Order, or support the wrestling tradition of World Championship Wrestling, the result Scott later announces is almost always the same: "One more for the bad guys!"

Tag Team Giants

Standing 6′ 8″ tall, Hall makes a fearsome duo with the 7′ Kevin Nash. As the Outsiders, these two have run roughshod over WCW, dominating tag team and singles matches inside the ring, and controlling the fate of the company outside it. No matter what combination you throw against them, it's very rare to see the Outsiders come out on the short end of a match. They're four-time WCW World Tag Team Champions, and should they ever set their sights on the tag team gold again, they'll have a fifth title in no time!

Proud to be "the bad guy," Hall breaks the rules and laughs in the face of authority. Despite this, he remains wildly popular with the fans and is mobbed by autograph seekers everywhere he goes. Some very public personal problems aside, including several blow-ups with his best friend and fellow Outsider, Kevin Nash, Hall always manages to come back stronger than ever before. On his way to becoming an all-time great, Scott Hall couldn't care less about the praise that's heaped upon him by the wrestling media. For Hall, the furor he has created by his own actions is reward enough.

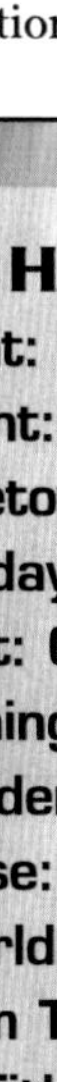

Scott Hall

- Height: 6′ 5″
- Weight: 280 lbs.
- Hometown: Miami, FL
- Birthday: October 20
- Debut: October 1984
- Finishing maneuver: Outsider's Edge
- Phrase: "Hey Yo!"
- Titles held: WCW World Television Title, WCW World Tag Team Title, WCW United States Title

World War III

Some of the most exciting matches in wrestling history have involved Scott Hall. He has declared himself the master of the ladder match, and his overwhelming record in this dangerous bout proves his claim is true. He's even overcome 60 other WCW superstars to become one of the few men to win the exhausting World War III battle royal. In that match, you could say he defeated the whole WCW company—in one night!

No Respect

Scott Hall's lack of respect for authority has become notorious in wrestling, but even that is not as bad as the disregard he has shown for the traditions of WCW. When WCW Commissioner Kevin Nash awarded Hall the WCW World Television Title, you would think that Hall would be happy to join in the legacy of former champions like Arn Anderson, Sting, and Lex Luger. Instead, Hall complained about having to carry around the belt and had Kevin Nash literally throw it into a trash can!

Outsider's Edge

While his partner, Kevin Nash, prefers to finish off opponents quickly with his Jackknife Powerbomb, Scott Hall likes them to think about their impending doom. For his "Outsider's Edge," Hall picks up his opponent for the bomb, then carries him across his back, holding him over his head by the arms, so that the poor guy's helpless to do anything but notice the height that he's been lifted to. Starting slowly, Hall falls forward, picking up speed as he ultimately drives his opponent's neck and shoulders into the mat.

nWo Nitro

May 27, 1996 was supposed to be one of the greatest days in WCW history. *WCW Nitro*, the revolutionary live wrestling television program, was broadcasting its first ever two-hour edition. Scott Hall, not under contract to WCW at that time, invaded the show and warned that things were about to change. Hall's arrival in WCW set the stage for what was to become the New World Order, a group that grew so powerful that at one point, it took over WCW's flagship program and called it *nWo Nitro*!

Daffney

She doesn't look like a model, and she couldn't care less. Daffney has only one thing on her mind and that's David Flair. She's an obsessed fan and totally in love with him. Screaming with joy when David brutalizes rivals with his crowbar, Daffney has been known to pull out a few wrestling moves of her own while interfering. Her real talent though seems to be her ear-splitting screams, which not only distract opponents, but can give them a real headache as well!

VALETS

In World Championship Wrestling, you will find some of the meanest, toughest men in the world. However, WCW does have a softer side, as it also includes some of the most beautiful women in the world. Wrestling can be brutal and vicious, and these ladies of the ring bring some much-needed grace and elegance to it. While some men think of them as no more than ornaments to wrestling, each of these women brings far more to the table than just a perfect body and a gorgeous face.

KIMBERLY

The wife of WCW champion Diamond Dallas Page, Kimberly has been a source of inspiration to DDP, who has credited her with much of his success. A force to be reckoned with, she's not afraid of facing up to much larger male wrestlers without backing down. Kimberly was also the driving force behind the Nitro Girls, the dance ensemble that performs at WCW TV events worldwide.

TORRIE

If you think Torrie Wilson looks like she should be a magazine cover girl, well, she is. This beautiful woman has graced the covers of many national fitness and health magazines, and her modeling career has taken her into commercials and TV shows. Once linked with Billy Kidman, she left him and moved onto The Franchise, Shane Douglas.

PAISLEY

She is almost as mysterious as the man she leads to the ring, but there is no mystery about her beauty. Paisley is the personal assistant to The Artist Formerly Known As Prince Iaukea. Her role is not only to attend to The Artist's needs at ringside, but also to serve as the spokeswoman for the reclusive and silent superstar.

MS. HANCOCK

A popular figure in WCW is the long-legged Ms. Hancock. Originally a member of Standards & Practices with Lane and Rave, she parted company with the duo when they declared her too "tightly strung" for their partying lifestyle. They should never judge a book by its cover. Ms. Hancock can let down her blonde hair and party with the best of them.

HEADLOCK

The headlock is perhaps the first wrestling hold ever invented and tends to be underrated. Whether applied with an opponent's torso from the front, the front facelock, or from behind, the side headlock, the principle remains the same. By simply adjusting the pressure on your opponent, you force him to expend energy trying to escape. In the meantime, the wrestler applying the hold is able to catch his breath and plot out his next move. The headlock can also be useful in slowing down the pace of a match, especially if you are facing an opponent like Rey Mysterio Jr., who prefers to fly rather than be drawn into a ground game.

JEFF JARRETT

He is the future of wrestling... at least that's what he tells people, and he may be right. Jeff Jarrett is a veteran despite his youth and certainly appears to have everything going for him to become the man that leads WCW. In fantastic shape, Jarrett can wrestle for hours without getting winded and can adapt to almost any style. Having spent years honing his craft before heading into WCW, he certainly has all the tools to justify his superstar status. One of those tools is his ego, which certainly has him convinced of his superiority to the rest of WCW. With the impressive array of wins he has under his belt, he is starting to convince the rest of the world as well.

His finishing maneuver, The Stroke, is a variation on a Russian legsweep. However, instead of taking an opponent backward, Jarrett drives them face first into the mat. No matter how big, tough, or quick you may be, Jarrett can find a way to beat you.

Jeff Jarrett hails from Nashville, Tennessee, home of some of the greatest country music in the world. Jarrett, however, seems to have found a different use for his favorite instrument, the guitar. Brandishing it as a weapon, Jarrett has used it to strum a violent tune across the backs of the heads of countless WCW stars, leaving them lying helpless in the ring. From what we hear, Jarrett doesn't even know how to play the thing!

SKULL BASHING

With all the confidence and ability in the world behind him, it's a shame that Jarrett feels the need to constantly break the rules and use underhanded tactics to obtain victories and keep the opposition down. Whether using the Harris brothers as muscle to bully a potential challenger to his status, or swinging his guitar to bash a rival's skull, Jarrett has shown that he will go to any lengths to maintain his role as the "Chosen One" of WCW.

JEFF JARRETT

- Height: 6' 1"
- Weight: 230 lbs.
- Hometown: Nashville, TN
- Birthday: July 14
- Debut: April 1986
- Finishing maneuver: The Stroke
- Phrase: "I am the Chosen One, slap nuts!"
- Titles held: WCW United States Title, WCW World Heavyweight Title

For almost an entire year, Jeff Jarrett worked to become a member of the Four Horsemen. He often said that his dream was to be part of the most elite group in wrestling history. After a long period of proving himself, Jarrett was finally given the chance by Arn Anderson and Ric Flair to raise the four fingers, the symbol of excellence. Ironically, Jarrett left the Horsemen less than a year later. He simply viewed getting into the Horsemen as a goal to be reached, and once he had accomplished it, he wanted greater challenges.

The versatility of Jeff Jarrett's repertoire is practically unmatched in this business. While closer in size to a cruiserweight than his larger opposition, the 5′ 10″, 230 pound Jarrett can bring the biggest rival down to the mat and stretch him from pillar to post.

CHOSEN ONE

Jeff Jarrett knew from the time he was a young child what he wanted to be. His father, Jerry Jarrett, is a legend in Tennessee, an area that is well-known for its support of professional wrestling. Jeff was around wrestling all his life, and his earliest childhood recollections revolve around the sport. In some ways, you could say that Jeff was born into wrestling. Maybe he truly is the Chosen One.

NEW WORLD ORDER

When the New World Order re-formed in the year 2000 it was expected to have a powerful core built around Bret Hart, Kevin Nash, Scott Steiner, and Jarrett. No one realized at that time that Jarrett would make a powerplay and look to take over the entire organization. Thanks to Jarrett, the nWo splintered once again, with him leading one faction and forcing his will on WCW. Instead of being a group, Jarrett's nWo was more like a private army, its sole focus being to carry out Jarrett's wishes.

KONNAN

He is one of the most popular yet controversial figures in the sport. He is a superstar in his homeland of Mexico, almost on a par with Hulk Hogan in the United States. He is Konnan, or K-Dawg, and whether it's as a wrestler, or as a personality, no one is more fascinating. It was he who opened the doors for other lucha libre stars to come to North America and display their talents. At the same time, he shattered the myth that all Mexican competitors are cruiserweights, unable to compete with the big boys of WCW. Throughout all of this, Konnan maintained a love-hate relationship with the fans, often breaking their hearts with his behavior, only to win them back later on.

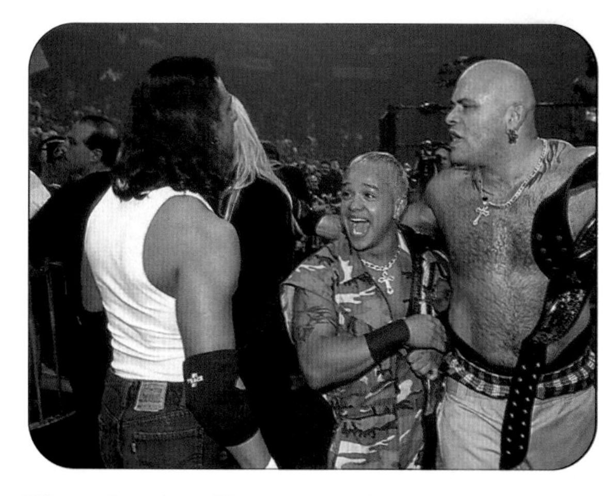

When choosing allies, Konnan has taken it to both extremes. He used to be a member of the Dungeon of Doom, a group that contained crazy brawlers like Hugh Morrus and Kevin Sullivan. Recently, he was a part of the Filthy Animals, which included Rey Mysterio Jr. and Billy Kidman. Konnan managed to fit into both groups perfectly.

Konnan's highly effective finishing hold, the Tequila Sunrise, is actually two different ones combined. First, he applies a spinning armlock, trapping the limb between his thigh and calf. Then, he pulls up his rival's leg in a half Boston crab. The result makes his poor opponent bend in half!

GANG MENTALITY

For a wrestler who has so much ability in the ring, you would think that Konnan would want to fight singles contests. Yet, for reasons known only to himself, Konnan prefers to be part of a group. Perhaps this dates back to his younger days when, in order to survive on the streets, you had to be part of a gang. His magnificent skill truly shines out in the ring. Beneath the street clothing and the gang mentality, he is a complete wrestler.

To say that Konnan is popular in Mexico is an understatement. He is a household name, appearing on TV and in the movies. WCW announcer Mike Tenay once recounted being in a restaurant in Mexico when Konnan appeared in a TV soap opera—and the place fell silent as everyone stopped to watch! Konnan even hosted a Spanish version of *Nitro*, called *WCW Latina*!

KONNAN

- **Height: 5' 10"**
- **Weight: 250 lbs.**
- **Hometown: Mexico City, Mexico**
- **Birthday: June 6**
- **Debut: 1987**
- **Finishing maneuver: Tequila Sunrise**
- **Phrase: "Arriba La Raza!"**
- **Titles held: WCW World Tag Team Title, WCW United States Title, WCW World Television Title**

La Parka

The skeletal costume La Parka wears is partially inspired by the Mexican holiday, "Day of the Dead." Held the same day as Halloween in the United States, this is one of the most popular days in the Mexican calendar and is cause for great celebration. In some ways you could say La Parka is like Santa Claus, except I don't think Santa has wrestled in too many hardcore matches!

Wearing a full bodysuit designed to look like a skeleton, you might think that La Parka is an overgrown Halloween trick-or-treater. But once you see this chair-swinging luchador in action, you'll realize that the trick is on his opponents. A multiple title holder in his native Mexico, La Parka was among the first luchadors to invade WCW when the company wanted to bring in top foreign talent from around the world. Establishing a cult popularity among fans, La Parka has become a regular on WCW programming, almost as much for his entertaining style as for his incredible ring skills.

"The Chairman of WCW," as he is often referred to, has turned the swinging of steel seats into a fine art. Combine that with his aerial ability and speed, and you have a lethal combination. However, there is much more to La Parka; he can convey a hilarious sense of humor without opening his mouth! He dances, struts, and makes fun of his opponent, all the while playing psychological games that will ease his route to victory. Of course, nothing makes that route easier than flattening an opponent with a chair to the head!

The Strut

The La Parka Strut, where the masked man climbs onto his chair and dances, is very popular among fans in the United States, and is absolutely worshiped in Mexico. Often, fans will wait for his strut with greater anticipation than the outcome of the match! It's definitely another thing that sets La Parka apart from everybody else, not just in WCW, but in all of wrestling!

How does one go about becoming the chairman of WCW? Do you get voted in by an executive board? Do you get elected by a jury of your peers? Or do you simply bring a steel chair to ringside, play it like an air guitar, stand on it and dance, and finally, use it as a weapon to knock out the opposition? If you picked the last one, you're correct!

La Parka

- Height: 6' 1"
- Weight: 235 lbs.
- Hometown: Mexico City, Mexico
- Birthday: December 11
- Debut: 1987
- Finishing maneuver: Chair to the head

CHICAGO
BLACKHAWKS
BIG
POPPA
PUMP

TOP ROPE

When you want to climb the ropes for a high-risk move, or set your opponent up for your finisher, you must accomplish two goals. First, stun your opponent. This gives you time to set up your move. Second, take him down quick and hard. Two good ways of accomplishing this are with the back body drop and the suplex. With the body drop, you whip your opponent into the ropes, and, as he rebounds at you, duck down and toss him over your shoulder. The suplex has more variations than we could begin to describe here, but the basic premise is simple enough. Suspend your opponent in the air, and send him crashing to the mat, leaving him stunned and in pain—a position that's the perfect target for your top rope move.

THE TOTAL PACKAGE

Many wrestlers can brag about being complete athletes, but there is only one "Total Package" in WCW, and that is Lex Luger. Almost 15 years after he first burst onto the scene, Luger is more impressive than ever, with a chiseled body that houses more power than a Mac truck. The difference between then and now is that these days Luger has a world of experience to go along with his athletic ability. A former member of the Four Horsemen, New World Order, and Wolfpac, Luger is constantly sought after by other wrestlers who are looking to gain an edge on the opposition. Then again, maybe they are just ensuring that they don't have to face the Package themselves!

If the Total Package has a perfect body, the lovely Elizabeth is his ideal match. This devil in disguise adds fuel to Luger's aggressive fire and often interferes in his matches with a baseball bat, or sprays opponents' faces with mace. The truth is, Luger doesn't need help to win, but this duo actually enjoys inflicting pain and leaving a trail of broken arms!

TEAM PACKAGE

One of the most celebrated rivalries in the history of wrestling is that of The Total Package and the Nature Boy. Lex Luger first faced Ric Flair in his rookie year, when Flair defended his world title against Lex, who was tearing up the wrestling scene in Florida. Since that time, the two have headlined countless shows, selling out arenas around the country. Through their rivalry, they developed mutual respect and recently formed "Team Package" with a very selective membership. It only has two wrestlers—them!

Alternately one of the most popular or most hated men in WCW, Luger's favor with the fans may change with every match, but the respect his opponents have for him never wavers. Lex Luger has been a dominant competitor from day one, and as long as the Total Package continues to find rivals to toss around the ring and break in half, he will continue to be one. With such musculature, it should come as no surprise that Luger was called "the next Hulk Hogan" during his early days in the sport. It was a tough tag to shake, but eventually Luger showed he was his own man. He permanently silenced the comparison forever when he defeated the Hulkster for the WCW World Heavyweight Title.

Mean Winning Streak

While success comes easily to Luger, he's never satisfied. The Total Package is a former WCW World Tag Team Champion, two-time WCW World Television Champion, five-time WCW United States Champion, and a two-time WCW World Heavyweight Champion. He has taken on and defeated the best the sport has to offer. Add in a genuine mean streak, and Luger becomes that much more dangerous.

Luger Disarms

Lex Luger and Sting broke into wrestling at the same time and formed what was thought to be a lifelong friendship. They were even in a successful tag team, winning the WCW World Tag Team Title. They've had their disagreements, even battling it out in the ring on occasion, but always patched things up eventually. It's hard to see how they will mend their most recent break, pun intended, as Luger broke Sting's arms by placing them in a steel folding chair and bashing it shut with a baseball bat!

The Total Package

- Height: 6' 4"
- Weight: 265 lbs.
- Hometown: Chicago, IL
- Birthday: June 2
- Finishing maneuver: The Torture Rack
- Phrase: "I am the Total Package"
- Titles held: WCW World Tag Team Title, WCW United States Title, WCW World Television Title, WCW World Heavyweight Title

Muscle Man

Three percent body fat. Let that sink in for a moment. Out of 265 pounds, less than 8 pounds of it is fat. Luger's dedication to physical fitness is truly remarkable. Even a motorcycle accident that forced him to have a steel plate implanted in his arm could not keep him from maintaining his body, which more closely resembles a Greek god's than a human's. Luger even considered a career in bodybuilding at one point and owns his own chain of gyms across the country.

MONDAY
NITRO
TNT

BERLYN

This Teutonic terror is one of the most perplexing characters ever to enter World Championship Wrestling. For five years, Alex Wright was the blond-haired high-flyer from Germany, looking more like a model than a bruiser. No one could have foreseen the change that would turn "Das Wunderkind" Alex Wright into Berlyn. The transformation came when Alex took a break from the ring to recover from an injury. When he returned, the blond hair was replaced with a black Mohawk and a sinister look. Wanting to be known as Berlyn, he now insists on speaking only German! Despite his antisocial attitude, he has maintained his in-ring skill, and his mean streak often gives him the edge.

Berlyn certainly has the right genes for wrestling. His father, Steven Wright, is one of the greatest European competitors ever. He has amassed so many titles and championships during his career, it would not be unfair to compare Steven to American greats like Ric Flair and Hulk Hogan. One has to wonder if the son is able to follow in the father's footsteps.

WITH THE WALL

When Berlyn finally decided he no longer needed a large entourage to protect him, he chose to keep The Wall around as his bodyguard. But when The Wall started to wrestle matches of his own, their relationship was over. Berlyn's ill-timed interference cost The Wall several matches, until finally the big man took down his employer with one of his patented Chokeslams!

Has the transformation to Berlyn helped this young man's career? Well, as Alex Wright, he did enjoy short reigns as WCW World Television Champion and WCW World Cruiserweight Champion. As Berlyn, he has yet to taste the gold, but with his newfound killer instinct, once he does have a strap, you can bet it will be more difficult to get it off of him!

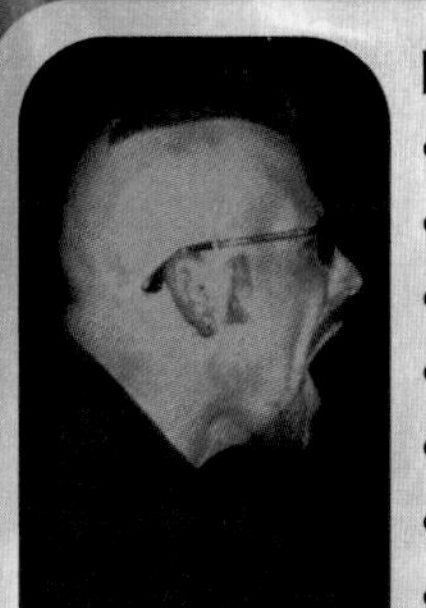

BERLYN
- Height: 6' 3"
- Weight: 230 lbs.
- Hometown: Nuremburg, Germany
- Birthday: May 17
- Debut: 1994
- Finishing maneuver: Neckbreaker
- Titles held: WCW World Television Title, WCW World Cruiserweight Title

The Wall

When the Berlin Wall was put up, many thought it would be there forever. When it was toppled, people called it a miracle. Well, a miracle is what it would take to bring down WCW's Wall. A monstrous sight to behold, this 6' 10", 320 pounds of solid mass has impressed many with how well he uses his size in the ring. Not the stereotypical "big man" people are used to in wrestling, The Wall more closely resembles competitors like Bam Bam Bigelow, who can move like lightweights, despite their girth.

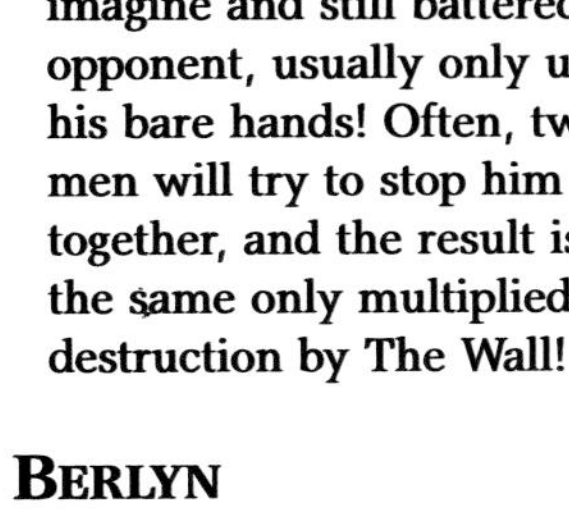

Can anything slow down The Wall? He's been in hardcore matches and taken every type of weapon shot you can imagine and still battered his opponent, usually only using his bare hands! Often, two men will try to stop him together, and the result is still the same only multiplied—destruction by The Wall!

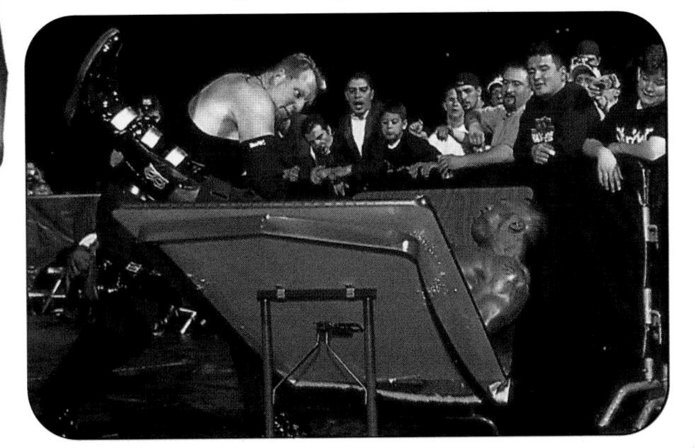

With Berlyn

The Wall's big break came in 1999 when he was hired by Berlyn as his bodyguard. While this brought him into the spotlight, he still looked to advance his own wrestling career, and that began the rift between the two. The Wall broke with his boss, and when Berlyn got physical over it, he learned the hard way how good his former bodyguard truly was!

Chokeslam

The Chokeslam is a powerful maneuver, but when The Wall puts his incredible strength behind it, the effect seems almost deadly. He's even created variations of the move, applying it from off the ropes to give it even more impact. On one occasion, he chokeslammed young Crowbar off the top rope and through the announcers' table during an edition of *WCW Thunder*, leaving Crowbar seriously injured. Even scarier than the incident itself was the fact that the Wall showed no remorse for his actions.

The Wall

- Height: 6' 10"
- Weight: 320 lbs.
- Hometown: Ocean Grove, NJ
- Debut: 1994
- Finishing maneuver: Chokeslam

THUNDER

Thunder, WCW's newest television offering, is entrusted to two of the most respected announcers in the business. "The Professor" Mike Tenay invokes his encyclopedic knowledge of the sport to provide play-by-play commentary on the action. Color commentary is handled by Bobby "The Brain" Heenan, who possesses, arguably, the most recognizable voice in wrestling, having been involved in the sport as an announcer and a manager for many years.

ANNOUNCERS

On top of all the wrestling action in WCW, there is another difficult task that needs to be accomplished. And that is to somehow describe all the action that is going on. Announcers certainly don't have it easy, and while their positions in WCW might not be the most glamorous, they are certainly among the most important. Most sports announcers could never keep up with the moves and holds the way the crack WCW announce teams do.

MEAN GENE

Probably the first wrestling household name to be produced in professional wrestling who is not a wrestler is "Mean Gene" Okerlund. The best interviewer in the business, hands down, Mean Gene has been delivering probing questions and getting straight answers for over two decades. Gene has even parlayed his fame into movie and television roles, where his trademark mustache and delivery are as recognizable as the red and yellow of Hulkamania.

NITRO

WCW's *Nitro* is hosted live every week by Tony Schivone and Mark Madden. Tony, a veteran play-by-play man, has called the action on WCW's programs for over 15 years, while Mark, his wisecracking sidekick, is a newcomer to the broadcast team. Madden, a former newspaper columnist and contributor to WCW's official website, WCW.com, has added a new spark to the show with his sarcastic wit and controversial opinions.

Hogan

There has never been, nor will ever be, a wrestler like Hogan. Unquestionably the greatest star ever produced by the industry, Hogan is responsible for the sport attaining unheard of popularity. He has become a household name even among those with only a passing interest in wrestling. Winning the WCW World Heavyweight Title on several occasions, Hogan has transcended the ring to become a media superstar, appearing on television and in motion pictures. Anything featuring Hogan, from shirts to toys, immediately sells out, and there is a constant demand for more merchandise featuring the "Immortal One."

It seems hard to grasp, but Hogan once seriously considered running for the highest office in the land. On an edition of the *Tonight Show with Jay Leno*, Hogan announced his retirement and his plans to campaign to be elected president of the United States! Considered to be a publicity stunt, Hogan shocked many when he actually did walk away from wrestling and seemed to be serious about his political future. However, the draw of the action proved to be too much for Hogan to resist, and he was soon back in the ring, where instead of signing bills to eliminate problems, you just throw punches!

First Heavyweight Title

He has defeated the best the sport has ever seen. Hulk Hogan beat Andre The Giant several years ago, bodyslamming him in the process, and took down Ric Flair to win the World Heavyweight Title in his first WCW pay-per-view. His brutal feud with Randy Savage saw Hogan get the better of the Macho Man time and time again, and the list of opponents that have fallen before the Immortal One is too long to even begin to recite. No matter the size or ability of the opposition, they all go down to the Hogan's world-famous mighty leg drop.

Although he could easily leave wrestling and live the luxurious life of a Hollywood star, Hogan always finds himself drawn back into the ring. He is responsible for the largest indoor crowd in the history of North America. More pay-per-view events have been headlined by Hogan than by any other wrestler. Even during the dark period of his history when he allowed his alter ego, Hollywood Hogan, to take over, he was still the top drawing card in the world.

Hogan
- Height: 6' 7"
- Weight: 275 lbs.
- Hometown: Venice Beach, CA
- Birthday: August 11
- Debut: 1978
- Finishing maneuver: Big Boot to the Face and Leg Drop
- Phrase: "What'cha gonna do when the Hulkster runs wild on you!"
- Titles held: WCW World Heavyweight Title

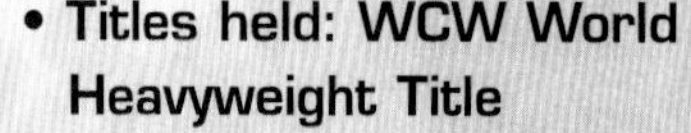

It was one of the darkest days in WCW history and opened a new chapter in Hogan's career. When Kevin Nash and Scott Hall took on Lex Luger, Randy Savage and Sting at *Bash At The Beach* on July 7, 1996, many believed that the Outsiders had been unable to find a partner. Over the course of the battle, Luger was injured, and Sting was knocked out cold, leaving only Savage at the mercy of Hall and Nash. When Hogan ran down the aisle, fans thought he was coming to save Savage. Instead, he dropped his leg across Savage's chest, and the New World Order was born.

Upon joining the New World Order, Hogan underwent a series of changes. His normal red and yellow were replaced with the nWo's black and white. He changed his name to "Hollywood Hogan," and he turned his back on his supporters. With a newfound mean streak, Hogan ran roughshod over anyone in his path, until he ran into two men who would take none of his attitude, Goldberg and Sting.

Golden Return

As time wore on, Hollywood Hogan seemed to fade, and the Hogan of old seemed to be shining through. As much as he tried to be evil, Hogan's natural sense of goodness slowly came back to the forefront. Looking at a world with no heroes, WCW needed Hulk Hogan back. Incredibly, it was Hogan's own son who told his father to return to his roots, and he did, donning the red and yellow and allowing Hulkamania to run free again. However, that was not the end of Hollywood Hogan, and the black and white has been seen on more than one occasion since its apparent demise.

Hall of Fame

Hogan's value to wrestling is hard to compare with anyone else in the industry. You need to look at other sports to find an equal. He is to wrestling what Ruth was to baseball, what Montana was to football, and what Jordan was to basketball. The difference is, Hogan's career has spanned far more years and shows no signs of slowing down. After all the battles, Hogan is still running wild.

DUSTIN RHODES

Another of WCW's second generation stars, Dustin Rhodes proudly states that he has taken the mantle of his father, Dusty Rhodes, and become the "American Dream 2000." If that is so, it's a sad reflection on what's become of the American way, as Dustin has taken to backstabbing and cheating as a means of getting ahead in the competitive world of professional wrestling. Often berating the fans and insulting those who once supported him, Dustin has confused and saddened those who cheered him on early in his career, when he showed an incredible work ethic to escape the formidable shadow of his father. Dustin says he could not care less what the fans think of him or his newfound attitude, as he is more concerned with settling old scores and taking care of business in the ring.

While a cocky swagger allied to brutal tendencies are Dustin's dominant characteristics, his ability in the ring is undeniable. He has a devastating lariat and one of the best bulldogs in the sport. His technical knowledge is balanced by his use of his fists in a brawl. Bending the rules is also no problem for this rough Texan.

DIRTY TACTICS

Although his technical skills are more than enough to earn him victories in the ring, Dustin is rather good at getting himself disqualified for illegal tactics—and one in particular. After stunning an opponent, Dustin will stretch his rival's legs across the ropes in the corner, leaving the poor guy's groin unprotected for a kick that would send a football 100 yards. While it costs him the match, Dustin seems pleased to hear his victim howl out in pain!

Dustin was lucky enough to be taken under the wing of wrestling star Terry Funk. The Funker even proclaimed Dustin to be more of a man than Dusty was. Sadly, Dustin took this as an insult to his father, and the Funk-Rhodes feud began. Dustin claimed that Dusty was every bit as hardcore as the legend from Amarillo ever was. He may want to talk to his old daddy soon; he might then learn that a fight with Funk is like a war against an indestructible soldier!

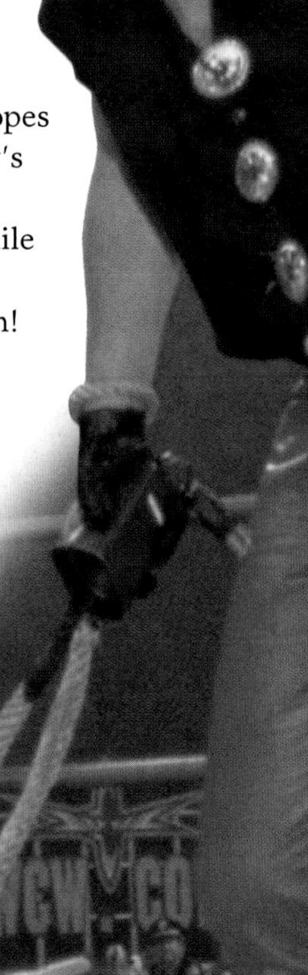

DUSTIN RHODES
- Height: 6' 5"
- Weight: 254 lbs.
- Hometown: Austin, TX
- Birthday: April 11
- Debut: Sept. 13, 1988
- Finishing maneuver: Bulldog
- Titles held: WCW World Six-Man Title, WCW World Tag Team Title, WCW United States Title

TERRY FUNK

TERRY FUNK
- Height: 6' 1"
- Weight: 247 lbs.
- Hometown: Amarillo, TX
- Birthday: June 30
- Debut: Dec 9, 1965
- Finishing maneuver: The Chicken Punch
- Titles held: NWA World Heavyweight Title, WCW Hardcore Title

There are few wrestlers who can be considered truly legendary. In the case of Terry Funk, however, there is no doubt about it. While the word legend usually recalls memories of past glories, Terry Funk is just as much a force in the sport now as he was 20 years ago, when he held the WCW World Heavyweight Title. "The Funker" is one of wrestling's living greats, and while he was known for his superb mat skills many years ago, he has stayed with the times and changed with them. He is a master of the hardcore match, and has no fears of going to the top rope and launching himself into a moonsault on the floor!

HARDCORE HERO

If ever a championship suited a wrestler, it's the WCW Hardcore Title and Terry Funk. Wrestling all over buildings, and even outside them, using any weapon he can get his hands on, is just a stroll through the park for the Funker. Chairs, ladders, and tables are the norm in his bouts. He'll use anything he sees, including trash cans, fire extinguishers, and even food to get the advantage over his rival. It only makes sense that Terry Funk has held the WCW Hardcore Title. After all, he practically invented the style to begin with!

Funk has actually retired on several occasions, but the pull of the ring and the desire to compete is just too strong. His most celebrated return came in 1989 when he attacked the then WCW World Champion Ric Flair, igniting one of the most violent feuds in the history of the sport. The wounds from that war ran so deep that, more than a decade later, there is still animosity between the two.

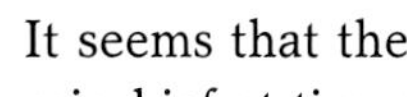

TROUBLEMAKER

It seems that the Funker can't help but get himself into mischief at times. In the late 1980s, television stations were nervous about the Funker coming on camera, for fear that he might say something that would get the channel into trouble. In the 1990s, he practically caused riots at shows in Japan as he brawled in the audience. In 2000, the legend caused major headaches for the management team of Vince Russo and Eric Bischoff. After all, here was an "old man" holding the WCW Hardcore Title in what was supposed to be the era of the "New Blood!"

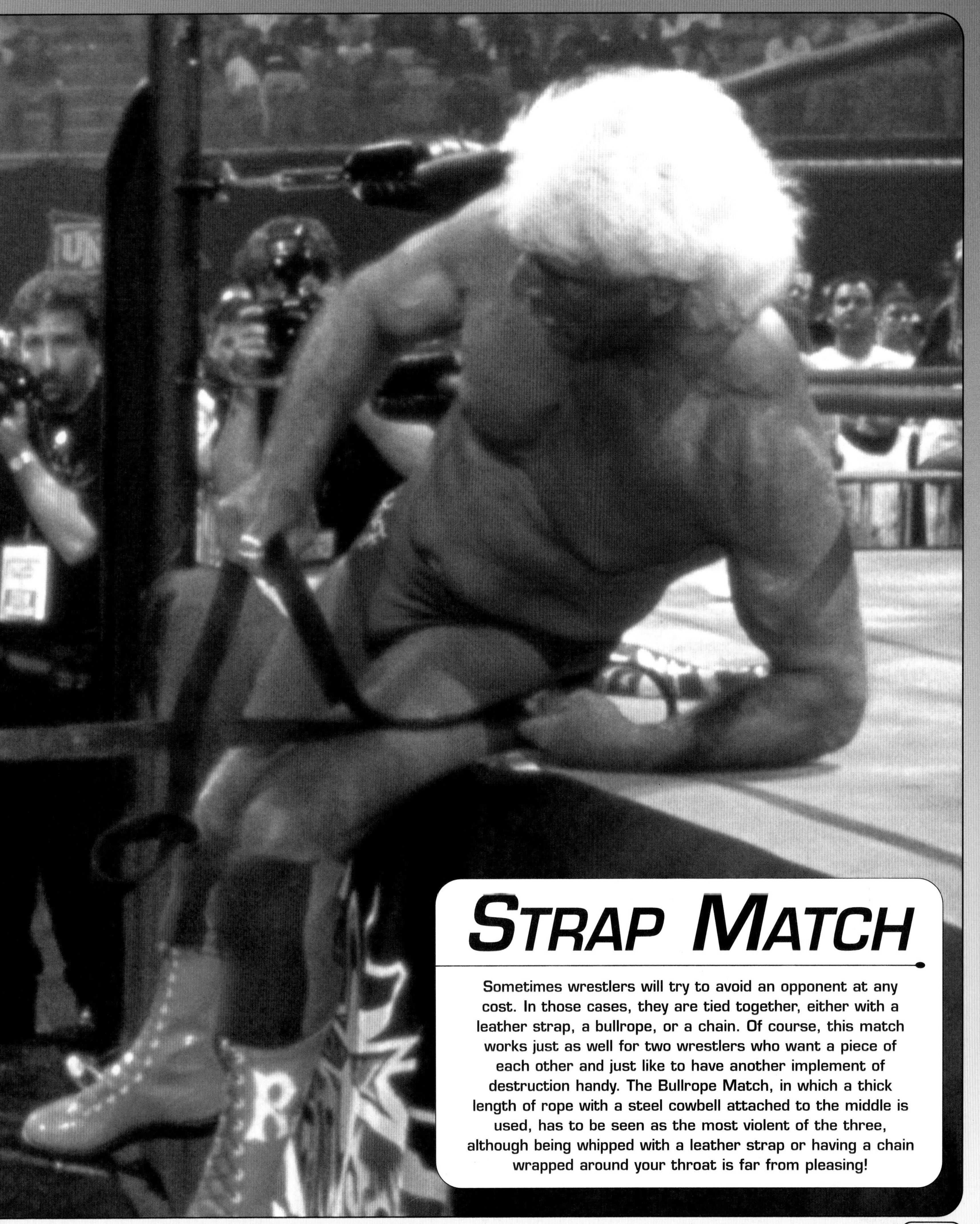

Strap Match

Sometimes wrestlers will try to avoid an opponent at any cost. In those cases, they are tied together, either with a leather strap, a bullrope, or a chain. Of course, this match works just as well for two wrestlers who want a piece of each other and just like to have another implement of destruction handy. The Bullrope Match, in which a thick length of rope with a steel cowbell attached to the middle is used, has to be seen as the most violent of the three, although being whipped with a leather strap or having a chain wrapped around your throat is far from pleasing!

BRET HART

The late Gorilla Monsoon christened Bret Hart the "Excellence of Execution," and the name has stuck over the years. As well it should, as Bret has mastered more holds and maneuvers than most competitors will ever use in their whole career. While Hart can outwrestle anyone on the mat, he certainly won't back away from a brawl either. He'll just as easily tie you in a pretzel, as he will knock your block off, all before making you submit to his trademark Sharpshooter.

He's "the best there is, the best there was, and the best there ever will be." Those words say it all about Bret "Hitman" Hart, perhaps the greatest pure wrestler ever to lace up a pair of boots. Universally respected by other wrestlers, Bret is almost as controversial as he is technically adept. Did he come to WCW to save it from the New World Order, or to join in nWo's destructive mission? Perhaps he did neither and simply came to the sport because he craved competition, and this is where he found the only talent that could challenge his abilities.

LORD OF THE RING

Bret has considered retirement several times in recent years. However, the pull of the ring remains strong and always draws him back. Bret is an incredible international draw, attracting standing room only crowds in every corner of the globe, in addition to being a national hero back home in Canada. Somehow he's managed to maintain his popularity the world over, balance several other careers and the demands of his family life, yet he continues to be successful at all he endeavors to achieve. Maybe pink and black aren't quite the right colors for Bret. Maybe he should be wearing the red and blue of Superman!

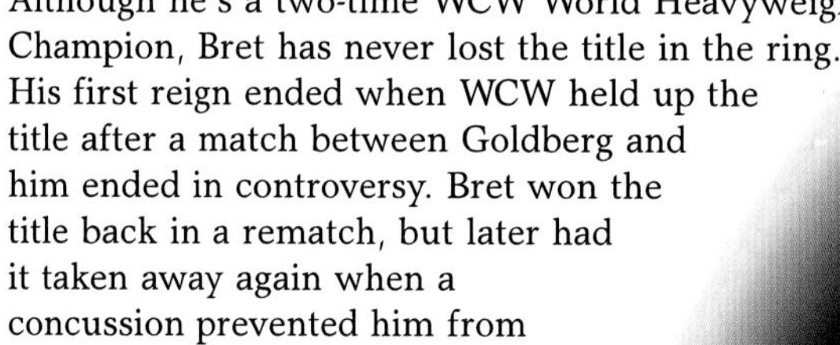

Although he's a two-time WCW World Heavyweight Champion, Bret has never lost the title in the ring. His first reign ended when WCW held up the title after a match between Goldberg and him ended in controversy. Bret won the title back in a rematch, but later had it taken away again when a concussion prevented him from defending the title.

BRET HART
- Height: 5' 11"
- Weight: 235 lbs.
- Hometown: Calgary, Alberta, Canada
- Birthday: July 2
- Debut: 1976
- Finishing maneuver: Sharpshooter
- Phrase: "The best there is, the best there was, and the best ever will be!"
- Titles held: WCW World Tag Team Title, WCW World Heavyweight Title, WCW United States Title

Bret Hart's first official appearance in WCW was not actually as a wrestler, but as a referee. Bret donned the striped shirt to officiate a match between Larry Zbyszko and Eric Bischoff to determine control of *WCW Nitro*, a match that Zbyszko won. Later that same night, he prevented the Hulk Hogan and the New World Order from "screwing" Sting out of the WCW World Title. Bret made an immediate impact that night, and he didn't even have to wrestle!

Careers Man

Although he's known as the Hitman perhaps a more fitting name would be the "Renaissance Man!" In addition to his busy wrestling career, Bret is also a cartoonist, an actor, and a weekly newspaper columnist. He is also the co-owner of his own hockey team, The Calgary Hitmen. What could be next for Bret, prime minister of Canada perhaps? Don't bet against it!

New World Order

Bret's on-again, off-again relationship with the New World Order has puzzled wrestling experts for several years. When he first made his intentions known that he was joining WCW, the nWo figured they would have a new ally. However, Bret didn't join immediately, and when he finally did, it was only for a short period. He has drifted in and out of the organization several times, leading many to believe that he is actually just looking to cause chaos and ultimately lead to the destruction of the group.

To say Bret comes from a wrestling background is perhaps the greatest understatement of all time. The son of wrestling legend Stu Hart, Bret and all of his brothers followed in their father's footsteps and became wrestlers. Even Bret's three sisters all married grapplers! You have to wonder if they need a referee when they get together for holidays!

CINERGY

CHRIS CANDIDO

Chris Candido may be the size of a cruiserweight, but his style is that of an all-around grappler. "Hard Knox" is a rugged mat wrestler in the tradition of Ric Flair, Terry Funk, and the Steiner brothers. Candido has the unique ability to make wrestlers play by his rules, grounding luchadors and drawing brawlers into technical combat that they can't hope to keep up with. A simple wrestler, Chris Candido doesn't need all the glitz and glamor that others require to make their presence known. All he needs is a ring and an opponent. He'll handle the rest.

Some say they're born to wrestle, but in Chris Candido's case, it's actually true! Candido's grandfather was "Popeye" Chuck Richards, an incredible grappler who spent years headlining in front of huge crowds. Chris himself starting training and helping to build rings at a young age, and by the age of 16 had already wrestled his first professional match. In fact, while most kids are graduating high school, Candido was already in title contention!

AMBITION

When Chris Candido entered WCW, he wasted no time in making it known that he was looking for championship gold. He quickly won his first belt, the WCW Cruiserweight Title, but certainly didn't have an easy time getting it. He had to defeat not one, but six men in a sudden death free-for-all, with bodies flying everywhere, and alliances being made and broken on a whim. Candido survived the battle, scored the victory with his Diving Headbutt, pinned The Artist, and brought home the gold.

No discussion of Chris Candido would be complete without acknowledging his stunning companion Tammy. One of the most popular women in the history of wrestling, Tammy has transcended the grappling world and crossed over into the land of mainstream celebrity. Of course, her stunning looks are only part of what she brings to the table. Fearless, Tammy will get right into the thick of things inside the squared circle, whether her adversary is a man or a woman!

CHRIS CANDIDO
- Height: 5' 8"
- Weight: 226 lbs.
- Hometown: Carteret, NJ
- Debut: 1986
- Birthday: March 21

MADUSA

While many women have openly bemoaned their treatment by the professional wrestling industry over the years, very few have actually shown the desire to step forth and change it themselves. Madusa is one of those few, challenging the "old school" style of thinking and showing that a woman can compete at championship level within the ring. She has inspired those who believe that women should not be ornaments to accompany male wrestlers, nor seen as freaks if they achieve professional excellence. No one is more responsible for the liberation of women in WCW than Madusa.

Madusa's first attempts at competing with men in the ring were not exactly the stuff of legend. She wrestled managers like Robert Parker and Paul E. Dangerously, who were certainly not championship caliber athletes. When she finally got a match with a wrestler, it did not go as she might have hoped. Her opponent was Meng, and the Tongan monster had no problem putting down his smaller rival. However, by being included in a tournament for the WCW World Title, Madusa had the distinction of being the first woman to compete for a male championship.

FEUDIN' FEMALE

Her matches with other female grapplers have often stolen the show, proving that their bouts can be just as exciting and well fought as the men's. It would seem that Madusa's oft-repeated call for a permanent women's division at WCW may be justified. If they do establish it, you can bet Madusa will be its first champion!

MADUSA

- **Height: 5' 9"**
- **Weight: 150 lbs.**
- **Hometown: Minneapolis, MN**
- **Finishing maneuver: German Suplex**
- **Phrase: "I want a women's division!"**
- **Titles held: WCW Cruiserweight Title**

LOVETRAP

When her physical ability couldn't get Madusa a chance to compete for the cruiserweight title, she instead decided to rely on her feminine charms. After helping Evan Karagias win the championship, she seductively coerced him into giving her a shot at the title. Blinded by love, Karagias agreed to the match and must now live with the fact that not only is the love affair over, but he is also the first man ever to lose a title to a woman in WCW history.

With her extensive knowledge of wrestling, it should come as no surprise that Madusa has also built up an impressive résumé as a manager. Although she now prefers to concentrate on her own career, in the past she has guided some of the true greats in the sport. At various times, she has managed Curt Hennig, Randy Savage, and others to great success and championships. The fact that she doesn't mind getting physically involved to help her man win has always been a plus as well!

THUNDER

The perfect compliment to *Nitro* is *Thunder*, another two-hour blast of WCW action, and in many ways the perfect buffer to its sister show. *Thunder* allows the wrestlers to regroup from the fallout of the previous *Nitro* or pay-per-view, and allows them to refocus their goals. It has also become known for providing more in-ring action than any program in the annals of wrestling broadcasting, as they go from match to match, with little time for filler.

Diamond Dallas Page

He once proclaimed "You love me, you hate me, but you'll never forget me"... and he was right. Diamond Dallas Page is many things, but he is certainly not forgettable. One of the most well-known wrestlers in the world, DDP has taken a most indirect route to the top, going from a hardly noticed manager, to commentator, to world champion. For someone who waited until his thirties to start actively competing, Page has put together a résumé that few will ever match. He doesn't possess the physique of Goldberg, nor does he have the incredible skill of Bret Hart, but he has managed to compete on their level through his sheer will and nerve.

Page is no stranger to Hollywood. He has appeared in television movies and has even had the honor of being a square on TV's *Hollywood Squares*!

Multi Title Star

Page certainly took an unusual road to find success, as most men start in the ring before moving on to managerial and announcing roles. DDP did it in reverse, but the method worked for him. Page has held all three major singles titles (WCW United States, WCW Television, and WCW World Heavyweight) in addition to the WCW World Tag Team Title. If he were lighter, he'd probably have won the WCW Cruiserweight Title as well!

Page Turner

Page is not only a championship wrestler, but quite a storyteller as well. He published a book called *Positively Page*, outlining the events of his life. From his days on the club scene of the Jersey shore, hanging out with the likes of Bon Jovi, to the start of his managerial career, all the way to his current success, it's an impressive record of experiences.

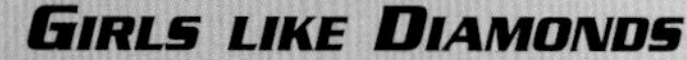

Girls like Diamonds

They say that behind every man is a good woman, and DDP certainly has a great one behind him. His wife Kimberly, the former Nitro Girl, is a constant source of inspiration and support to her man. Of course, if anyone messes with his lady, they will soon feel Page's wrath! Kimberly can take care of herself, but Page has no problem using the Diamond Cutter on anyone who causes her problems!

DDP has a shifty side to him, and he certainly knows how to plot a situation to his advantage. He formed the New Jersey Triad with Bam Bam Bigelow and Kanyon, solely to make sure he could maintain a grasp on the WCW World Tag Team Title.

DDP's feud with Hulk Hogan certainly led him into a pair of unusual tag teams. He even teamed up with NBA great Karl Malone to battle Hogan and Dennis Rodman, and later tagged with *Tonight Show* host Jay Leno to defeat Hogan and Eric Bischoff.

DIAMOND DALLAS PAGE

- Height: 6' 5"
- Weight: 253 lbs.
- Hometown: Point Pleasant Beach NJ
- Birthday: 5 April
- Finishing maneuver: The Diamond Cutter
- Phrase: "Feel the Bang!"
- Titles held: WCW World Tag Team Title, WCW United States Title, WCW World Heavyweight Title, WCW World Television Title

TOO HARD TO CUT

It is one of the most imitated maneuvers in wrestling. Diamond Dallas Page unveiled the Diamond Cutter early in his career and has countless methods of applying it. Victory is practically guaranteed when he hits the move, and you can probably count on one hand the number of stars who have kicked out of it!

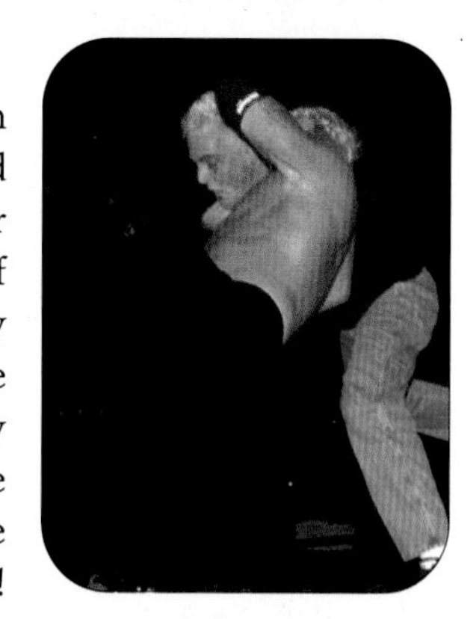

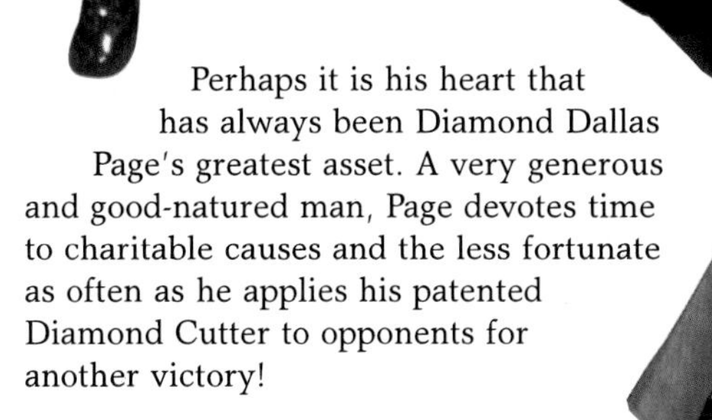

Perhaps it is his heart that has always been Diamond Dallas Page's greatest asset. A very generous and good-natured man, Page devotes time to charitable causes and the less fortunate as often as he applies his patented Diamond Cutter to opponents for another victory!

CHAMPION

Diamond Dallas Page's long journey to the WCW World Heavyweight title finally ended on April 11, 1999 when he overcame not only champion Ric Flair, but also Sting and Hulk Hogan in a four-way match. He didn't have it any easier when he won it a second time, overcoming Sting, Kevin Nash, and Bill Goldberg to win back the title he had lost earlier that evening to Sting. Maybe someday Page will be allowed to take it easy and just wrestle one man for the title!

Tank Abbott

Not since Goldberg has anyone made such an immediate impact in WCW. Tank Abbott, a superstar from the world of Ultimate Fighting has crossed over into the ranks of professional wrestling very smoothly. Of course, that's the only thing about Tank that is smooth, as his style is brutally rough, and absolutely relentless. In the world of Ultimate Fighting, no holds are barred, and you can use any means necessary to destroy your opposition. Tank came to WCW with the same mindset, but realizing he needed to strengthen points of his game, wisely kept his rough side in reserve!

Meng. The Barbarian. Jerry Flynn. What do these names have in common? Two things. One, they are among the toughest men, not only in WCW, but in the entire world. Two, they have all been knocked out by Tank Abbott. The list of tough guys to fall at the hands of Tank just keeps getting longer and longer.

Brawler Behind Bars

How brutal is Tank Abbott? Well, prior to entering the world of Ultimate Fighting, Tank spent some time in one of United States' fine rehabilitation facilities. In other words, he was in prison. In fact he was selected by the Ultimate Fighting organizations because they wanted to show the superiority of trained martial artists against barroom brawlers. Well, that experiment didn't quite work, as Tank vanquished opponent after opponent, until there was nothing left for him to accomplish there.

Battle Tank

Rather than rush headlong into the title hunt of May 1999 when he made his debut, Tank enrolled into WCW's Power Plant training facility. There, under the guidance of legendary veteran Bobby Eaton, Tank went from being a bone-crushing machine to a polished pro grappler. If Tank was threatening before, he was practically unstoppable now. Tank showed the whole world that he had the bravado to match his skills, challenging anyone in the company to take him on. While most newcomers are content to work their way up by battling other rookies, Tank instead lunged headfirst into matches with some of the toughest this sport has to offer, and incredibly, came out victorious every time. In only a few short months, Tank has secured a place in the upper echelon of WCW, and he doesn't plan on leaving anytime soon.

Bold Challenge

In the history of the WCW World Heavyweight title, no wrestler has come as close to tasting the gold with such little experience behind him as Tank Abbott. Granted a title match against then champion Sid Vicious, Tank brutalized the titleholder with body punches, before tossing him down, looking for the knockout punch. Only Sid's years of experience saved him from certain defeat, but a message was sent loud and clear that night. Tank Abbott, on any given night, could challenge for any title in wrestling.

How do you make an immediate impact in WCW? Well, you can start by targeting one of the most popular stars in wrestling. That's what Tank did when he attacked Sting. Tank had been selected to act as referee for a Steel Cage match between Sting and Rick Steiner. With his background, Tank was a natural to control the bout. Instead, he took it as an opportunity to level Sting and immediately see his name in wrestling headlines.

Duel of Honor

Shortly after beginning to compete full-time in WCW, a former member of Tank's entourage in Ultimate Fighting, Big Al, began appearing at ringside during his matches. Al accused Tank of selling out his no-holds-barred fighting reputation to compete in wrestling. Tank, looking to shut up his former friend, challenged him to a "skins match," where Tank's leather jacket, and more importantly, his pride, were put on the line. The jacket was placed on a pole, and after destroying Big Al, Tank climbed up and reclaimed it, with his honor intact.

Tank is very proud of all he accomplished in Ultimate Fighting and plans to achieve similar success in WCW. However, after witnessing his brutality in the ring, you would be shocked to discover that Tank is very soft-spoken outside the ring. Confident and determined, Tank doesn't need to yell and scream to make his point. His actions in the ring speak louder than words ever could.

Tank Abbott
- Height: 6'
- Weight: 265 lbs.
- Hometown: Huntington Beach, CA
- Finishing maneuver: Knockout Punch

THUNDER

BATTLE ROYAL

Throw two WCW stars in the ring, and you are guaranteed excitement. Throw in a few more, and things get very interesting. However, if you fill a ring with top-notch athletes, you have the makings for total chaos. That's exactly what happens in a Battle Royal. Alliances are made and then suddenly broken, and no one is safe, as 10, 20, or even 30 men battle it out at once. Elimination only occurs when you are thrown over the top rope to the cold, unforgiving floor below. While this type of match would seem to favor the bigger, stronger competitors, it is sometimes the crafty wrestler who is able to manipulate the madness and claim the victory.

SID VICIOUS

From the day he first set foot into a WCW ring, the world knew that wrestling's future had arrived, and his name was Sid Vicious. Originally one half of a devastating tag team called the Skyscrapers, it was inevitable that this 6′ 8″ powerhouse would go even higher on his own and take his rightful place as one of the sport's top stars. Experts dubbed him "the next Hulk Hogan" when he first broke into the sport, but he has gone on to carve a niche all of his own. If ever a powerhouse like this graces WCW again, he'll probably be referred to as the "next Sid Vicious!"

Although he prefers to rely only on himself now, Sid spent his formative years in the business as part of a team. Initially, he was one half of the Skyscrapers tag team with fellow giant Danny Spivey. Later, he was recruited by Ole Anderson to be a member of the legendary Four Horsemen, along with Barry Windham, Arn Anderson, and Ric Flair.

CONTROLLED POWER

Intelligent, yet crazy, mad, yet calculating, Sid may best be compared to a nuclear reactor. He is a bundle of energy that can always explode, but instead is properly controlled for maximum effectiveness. If you want to know how effective, just ask the slew of opponents who have found themselves staring at the ring lights after receiving his massive chokeslams or devastating powerbombs. Of course, you won't be able to ask them right away, as Sid's opponents are often unconscious afterwards! One victim describes the experience like this. "The first thing you see is the ceiling coming at you. Then you start going the other direction really fast. Then it hurts. It hurts bad."

SID VICIOUS

- Height: 6′ 8″
- Weight: 318 lbs.
- Hometown: Marion, AK
- Birthday: July 4
- Debut: 1987
- Finishing maneuver: Powerbomb
- Phrase: "I am the master, and the ruler of the world!"
- Titles held: WCW World Heavyweight Title, WCW United States Title

Most wrestlers rely on one move to ensure them of victory, and they build their whole strategy towards setting up their opponent for it. Sid actually has two effective finishers and can apply either at any time. His chokeslam, where he grasps his opponent around the neck and lifts him straight up, only to bring him crashing down, can end a match in an instant. However his personal favorite is the powerbomb, and when Sid plants his rival with it, the referee can count to a hundred and there still won't be a kickout! More recently, he has added a third finisher, the crossface, which is a move that causes such pain that an opponent is forced to tap out within seconds of the hold being applied.

When Sid Vicious finally reached the pinnacle of the sport and won the WCW World Heavyweight Title, he had no idea he'd have to win it twice to keep it! After defeating Kevin Nash for the vacant title, Nash abused his power as WCW Commissioner and awarded the belt to himself. Sid ended up having to defeat Nash and Ron Harris in a steel cage to win back the title that was rightfully his.

The Intimidator

There is an old saying in wrestling: if you can intimidate your opponent, then you've already won half the battle. Well, Sid must always come into the ring halfway to victory, because he is a master of intimidation! He has been known to laugh right in the face of his opponents, then stare them down with a steely gaze that could make even the toughest man tremble in his boots. Then, after all that, the bell rings and you actually have to wrestle him!

Who is the Future?

Who is the future of WCW, Sid or Goldberg? Well, the answer is not an easy one. When they did battle for the first time, Goldberg was declared the winner when it was ruled that Sid had lost too much blood in their match for the WCW United States Title. This led to an "I quit" rematch, where Goldberg was again victorious, but only because Sid was rendered unconscious. To date, Goldberg has been unable to pin or force a submission from Sid. They could battle a hundred more times, and we may still never have a decisive winner!

ROWDY RODDY PIPER

He is, without question, the greatest wrestler never to win the WCW World Heavyweight Title. Rowdy Roddy Piper is a famous figure in the sport and one of the two men most responsible for the popularity of professional wrestling today—the other being his lifelong rival, Hulk Hogan. In Piper's own words to Hogan, "Would they have loved you so much, if they hadn't hated me?" But the man fans loved to hate would eventually go on to become one of the best-loved figures in wrestling. For a while Piper left the sport to pursue his acting career and charitable work, but returned when he saw the New World Order trying to destroy WCW. The Rowdy Scot put up a fight and was the first to expose chinks in the nWo armor.

LEGENDARY MATCH

In the fabled feud of Piper vs. Hogan, and all the incredible battles they've waged, only once have they fought to a decisive finish. There were always disqualifications and outside interference, and neither one ever had the satisfaction of cleanly defeating the other, until *Starrcade '96*. Although Hogan refused to put his world title on the line in the match, there was something far more valuable on the line: the bragging rights of being the victor of the most celebrated feud in wrestling history. After battering each other from pillar to post, Roddy Piper did what no one else had ever done. He put Hulk Hogan to sleep, rendering him unconscious in the center of the ring! Rowdy Roddy Piper had won the war.

ROWDY RODDY PIPER
- Height: 6'
- Weight: 235 lbs.
- Hometown: Glasgow, Scotland
- Birthday: April 7
- Debut: 1972
- Finishing maneuver: Sleeper Hold
- Phrase: "I Cower Over Nothing!"
- Titles held: WCW United States Title

THE OLD GUARD

"I scare Flair." Well, if Ric Flair was going to be afraid of anyone, Roddy Piper would be a good choice. These two have had a unique relationship over the years, going back and forth between being partners and enemies. Truth is, they are among the last of the old guard of professional wrestling, and while Piper seems to want to pave the way for the next generation, Flair is more obsessed with achieving personal glory.

You never know when Roddy Piper will strike, or what role he will appear in. As he is fond of saying, "Just when you think you have all the answers, I change the questions." Whether it's smacking around authority figures, or stretching out opponents in the ring, Piper has always done things his way. While time and injuries (he wrestles with a titanium hip) have slowed him down somewhat, you can always expect a good fight out of ol' RP, since most of the time his rivals are rendered unconscious!

HACKSAW JIM DUGGAN

In an age when heroes are hard to find, it's good to know there's always one man you can count on. Hacksaw Jim Duggan has been fighting the good fight for many years, and he's still going strong. One of the most fondly regarded stars in the sport, his trademark cry of "Hoooo!" echoes through every venue where WCW holds an event. A patriot who fights for what he believes in, Hacksaw is as American as apple pie and not ashamed to admit it. The only thing bigger than his huge right hand punches is his heart. Hacksaw is truly the people's champion.

While most wrestlers fight for money or personal glory, Duggan does battle for a more noble cause. He fights for his country and always brings Old Glory into the ring with him. In fact, nothing and no one will ever make Duggan renounce his country. He believes in America, the same way the fans believe in him.

USA... USA... USA... USA...!

Of course, he's also been a championship wrestler as well, but if you ask ol' Hacksaw, he'll tell you that the chants of "USA" from the fans and the support that they've given him over the years mean more than any gold belt ever could. Duggan has a strong appreciation for the great history of wrestling and is one of the first to step in when that history is threatened by wrestlers with more selfish motives. Wrestling will always need someone like Hacksaw Jim Duggan, if for no other reason than to remind us that there is still good left in the world. If you fight the good fight, then even in defeat, you have already won. Hacksaw Jim Duggan is always a winner.

HACKSAW JIM DUGGAN
- Height: 6' 3"
- Weight: 280 lbs.
- Hometown: Glens Falls, NY
- Birthday: Jan 14
- Debut: Sept. 1977
- Finishing maneuver: Running Clothesline Tackle
- Phrase: "Hoooooo!"
- Titles held: WCW United States Title, WCW World Television Title

Why does Hacksaw bring a 2 x 4 into the ring? Well, as Hacksaw once explained, he's not about being "fancy dancy." He's just plain old Hacksaw, so what better weapon to use than a plain old piece of lumber? Of course, it may just be a board, but you can ask all the opponents who have been on the receiving end of it and they'll tell you, it doesn't have to be "fancy dancy" to hurt!

CHICAGO
BLACKHAWKS
CENTER

CLOTHESLINE

The clothesline appears to be a very simple move to execute. Whip your opponent into the ropes and as he rebounds toward you, extend your arm and catch him across the chest, as if he had run into a clothesline (hence the name). However, many a wrestler has ripped his bicep by hitting the clothesline incorrectly. You must be sure to catch the opponent with all of your arm, otherwise you risk injury. Variations on the clothesline, including leaping off the top rope for a flying version, require that the same basic principle be applied.

REFEREES

WCW's senior referee is Nick Patrick, and with his position, he has probably been in the ring more than any two or three wrestlers combined! His toughest night as a referee came when, as part of the nWo, he had to officiate every match on their *Souled Out* pay-per-view event. He barely lasted that night, but being the referee for the majority of WCW's main events, Patrick is used to being banged around. And, unlike a baseball umpire, he doesn't get to wear pads and a mask!

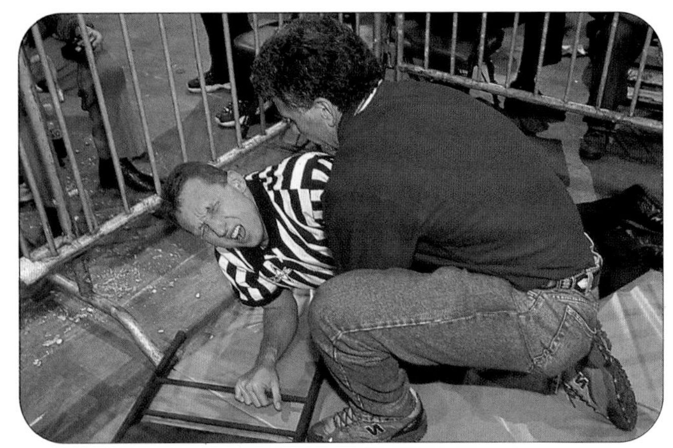

While referees are supposed to be unbiased and never favor one wrestler over another, you can't tell them not to have favorites outside of the ring. In the case of referee Charles Robinson, he is the ultimate Ric Flair fan. In fact, he is such a devotee of the Nature Boy that his nickname is "Lil' Naitch." Robinson even aligned himself with Flair during The Nature Boy's time as president of WCW. He was also the referee for Ric Flair's final world title victory over Hulk Hogan.

Sometimes referees get into disputes over how each other may call a match. Sometimes decisions are even reversed. On one occasion, two referees decided their differences could only be settled in the ring! Mark Johnson, who openly stated that he was a "referee that could be bought," accepted payoffs from the nWo to make calls in their favor. This infuriated veteran official Mickey Jay so much that he demanded the chance to face Johnson in the ring. Mickey won the match, but we all think he's much better off being an official. He's no Goldberg!

Sting

He is the franchise player of WCW, and perhaps no one better represents the organization than the man called Sting. He has truly become one of the top stars in the sport. Breaking into the business alongside the Warrior, Sting was originally seen as no more than a face-painted muscleman, but soon stunned crowds with his displays of agility and speed. He worked his way up the ladder of WCW at a breakneck pace and rapidly became a huge star, even though he had only just begun to fulfill his potential. He was soon collecting titles like a kid collects baseball cards, defeating Hulk Hogan to become a six-time World Heavyweight Champion and holding onto no less than five different championships on 14 separate occasions.

On March 27, 1988, in Greensboro, NC, WCW held the first-ever *Clash of the Champions* event, where the young Sting got his first chance at greatness. He challenged Ric Flair for the WCW World Heavyweight Title in an incredible 45-minute bout. Sting didn't walk home with the gold that night, but everyone saw that a new star had been born.

Scorpion Deathlock

Many wrestlers have one or two effective finishing moves, but few have three! Sting has been using the Stinger Splash since early in his career, whipping opponents into the turnbuckle, then sandwiching them with a leaping bodypress. He later developed the Scorpion Deathlock, which is responsible for many of his championship victories. In more recent years, he has begun to rely more on the Scorpion Death Drop, a reverse DDT that can render even the biggest foe unconscious on impact.

Image Makeover

After years of being among the most colorful competitors in the sport, Sting underwent a tremendous change in appearance. The blond crewcut, brightly painted face, and exuberant attitude were replaced with a darker, brooding look, and a mysterious attitude. However, when the adrenaline starts pumping in his veins, he is still the same old Stinger, beating his chest and yelling to his legions of fans. Although he has found a fruitful second career in acting, it's unlikely that Sting will ever fully leave the ring lights for the fantasy world of movies. He loves wrestling far too much, and wrestling fans love him right back.

Famous Feuds

Most wrestlers are remembered for their moves, but with Sting, you could spend hours recounting his memorable feuds. His matches with Ric Flair are the stuff of legend, and who can forget the war he waged to win back WCW from the nWo and Hollywood Hogan, or his on-off feud with Lex Luger. Truth is, Sting never does anything halfheartedly, and when he becomes embroiled in a fight, there's no stopping him until the matter is settled.

WCW Avenger

When the New World Order used a fake Sting to trick Lex Luger, the real Stinger found himself accused of being a traitor by his fellow WCW wrestlers. No one would believe Sting, so he decided he would no longer be involved in WCW's war with the nWo. He took to watching the matches from the upper reaches of the arena and held true to his word about not getting involved. When all seemed hopeless for WCW, that's when he returned, dramatically, by attacking from the rooftop and taking out the enemies of World Championship Wrestling one by one.

Looking over his win-loss record, you have to be impressed by the names Sting has defeated over the years in championship matches—Hulk Hogan, Steve Austin, Ric Flair, and Vader. His most bittersweet championship, however, came on April 26, 1999 during a live edition of *WCW Nitro*. After defeating Diamond Dallas Page for the world title early in the evening, he later placed it on the line in a four-way match with DDP, Kevin Nash, and Hulk Hogan. Unexpectedly, DDP won back the title, which put Sting in the record books for the shortest WCW World Title reign ever, lasting less than two hours!

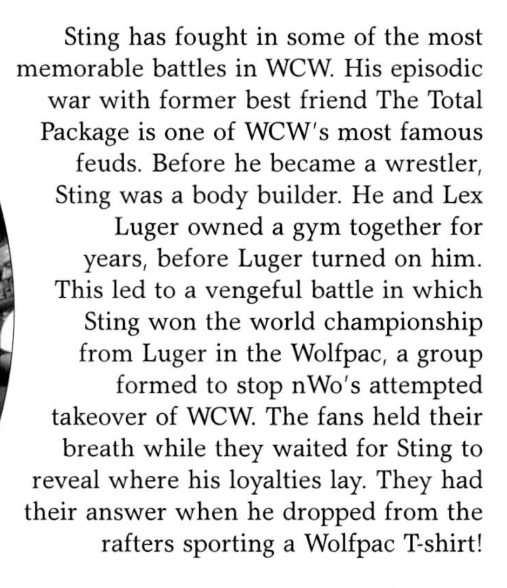

Sting has fought in some of the most memorable battles in WCW. His episodic war with former best friend The Total Package is one of WCW's most famous feuds. Before he became a wrestler, Sting was a body builder. He and Lex Luger owned a gym together for years, before Luger turned on him. This led to a vengeful battle in which Sting won the world championship from Luger in the Wolfpac, a group formed to stop nWo's attempted takeover of WCW. The fans held their breath while they waited for Sting to reveal where his loyalties lay. They had their answer when he dropped from the rafters sporting a Wolfpac T-shirt!

Victory over Evil

The pinnacle of the war between WCW and the nWo, and the match that would set the course for wrestling in the future, took place at *Starrcade '97*. It was the epic showdown between Sting and Hollywood Hogan, and despite the New World Order trying every trick in the book, they couldn't change the inevitable, and Sting defeated Hogan to win his sweetest WCW World Heavyweight Title. The ring filled with members of the WCW roster celebrating Sting's amazing victory over the evil organization.

Sting

- Height: 6' 2"
- Weight: 252 lbs.
- Hometown: Venice Beach, CA
- Birthday: March 20
- Debut: 1985
- Finishing maneuver: Scorpion Death Lock
- Phrase: "Owwww!"
- Titles held: WCW United States Title, WCW World Heavyweight Title, WCW International Title, WCW World Tag Team Title, WCW World Television Title

VAMPIRO

He is as mysterious as the night itself. Vampiro is the type who likes to keep himself to himself most of the time. He's rarely seen in daylight, and on the rare occasions he does make contact, he usually has a specific purpose in mind. Looking more like a character from a horror movie than a human being, Vampiro's unusual demeanor and exciting ring style have made him a cult favorite among the legions of WCW supporters. Although he has formed brief alliances in the past, he has survived as a loner in a business where who you know is sometimes as important as what you can do.

Before becoming a wrestler, Vampiro worked as a bodyguard for some of the biggest rock bands in the world. And his link with music didn't stop when he entered the ring. WCW announcer Mike Tenay discovered that one of Vampiro's favorite hobbies is performing as the lead singer in his own punk rock band!

MYSTERY MAN

After years of being sought after by organizations all over the world, Vampiro finally decided to curb some of his nomadic tendencies by settling in World Championship Wrestling. Here he felt there was sufficient talent for him to test the skills he had honed night after night. Still, some things remain a mystery about this man. Why the dark, brooding attitude, the ghostly facepaint, dragon tattoos, and leather ring gear? Do they have a special significance? Is this how Vampiro truly is, or is it just part of an elaborate ruse to gain a psychological advantage over opponents? Whatever motivates him, Vampiro is a superstar with the potential to become one of the leaders of WCW in the new century.

AGAINST BERLYN

An early feud in Vampiro's career saw him butting heads with another young upstart; Alex Wright, a.k.a. Berlyn. Vampiro lives the lifestyle of his dark and brooding image, and he saw Berlyn as a phony, trying to portray a gothic lifestyle that the German knew nothing about. The two settled their differences in a brutal chain match.

VAMPIRO
- **Height: 6' 1"**
- **Weight: 240 lbs.**
- **Hometown: Thunder Bay, Ontario**
- **Finishing maneuver: Nail in the Coffin and Vampiro Spike**

The Future of Fight

Whenever Vampiro steps into the ring to do battle with Kidman, they should probably bill it as "the Battle for the Future." These two young stars are the future of this organization and will most likely be headlining shows around the country for many years to come. Although they have teamed on occasion, mostly due to mutual respect, they are far more entertaining when they are on opposite sides of the ring.

In one of the more unusual feuds ever to take place in WCW, Vampiro found himself embroiled in a series of debacles with the decidedly nonathletic announcer, Oklahoma. Somehow, the two kept interfering in each other's plans and, before long, they realised that the only way to settle their differences was in the ring. The results were not pretty, and the world found out that Oklahoma should have stuck to announcing—he had no chance in the ring with Vampiro!

Respect

While some wrestlers complain about not being afforded sufficient respect by the industry's veterans, few have the courage to do anything about it. Vampiro is one of those few and has shown tremendous faith in his abilities by challenging top performers like Ric Flair and Jeff Jarrett. He may not always come out victorious, but with every match Vampiro gains a little more respect form the old guard. Eventually, he will be the man rookies look to get respect from.

Individual Style

Although he comes from Canada, Vampiro's style is decidedly out of tune with that of other competitors from up north, like Bret Hart. Instead he presents a mix of Mexican lucha libre, and martial arts kicks and thrusts. His finishing moves, the Nail in the Coffin and the Vampiro Spike, were perfected after years of competing north and south of the United States before he finally entered the competitive scene of WCW.

SUPLEX

The suplex is a deceptive maneuver. While many wrestlers learn it early in their careers, it can take a lifetime to master. The standard vertical suplex begins by placing your opponent in a front facelock, then draping his arm around your own neck. Using that as your point of leverage, you hook the opponent's trunks and pull back, lifting him into the air, upside down and parallel to your body. After allowing a few seconds for the blood to rush into his head (Ric Flair is well known for keeping an opponent upside down for an extended period), you fall back, sending them crashing to the mat on their back.

JERRY FLYNN

With Flynn's martial arts skills, it was natural that he should enter a match with three-time world karate champion Ernest "The Cat" Miller. The two have done battle on several occasions, and Flynn regards his several victories over Miller as among the highlights of his WCW career. Thankfully, Jerry has stuck to wrestling The Cat and never tried to out-dance him!

The wrestling business almost has a language of its own, full of terminology the average person wouldn't understand. One such term is "shooter." In the old days, when a promoter was having trouble with a particular wrestler, he would match that person up against a shooter—someone who could more than handle himself in any type of fight. You could say that the shooter is someone the other wrestlers regard as being among the toughest in the company. He's the kind of person who will just as easily tie you in a pretzel in the ring, as he would knock your head off in a streetfight! A shooter is someone you don't want on your bad side. Jerry Flynn is one such shooter.

THUNDERFOOT

"Thunderfoot," as Flynn likes to be called, commands respect from wrestlers and fans alike. Trained in several disciplines of the martial arts, Jerry mixes his skill with the more traditional wrestling mat techniques to form a hybrid style that is uniquely his own. It's also a lethal combination that gives him a clear advantage over opponents unschooled in the ancient fighting arts. They rarely know what's hit them!

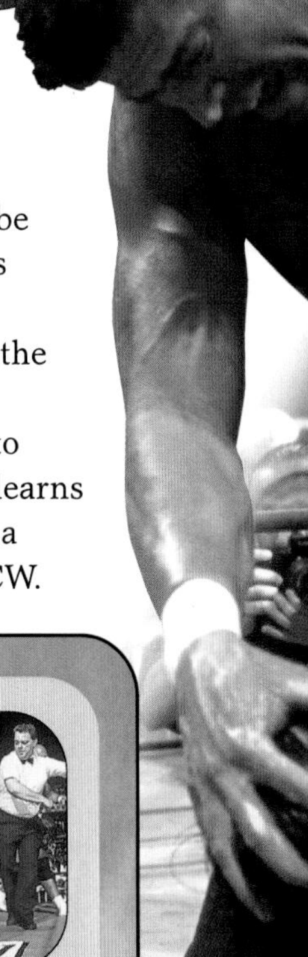

THE FUTURE

Impressive credentials abound with Flynn, so one has to wonder why he's not had more championship success in WCW. Perhaps it can be traced to his temper. When provoked, he allows his mental discipline to take a backseat, and it often costs him matches. Either he will cross the line and get disqualified, or he loses concentration, allowing a crafty opponent to outsmart him and score the victory. If he learns to keep his temper in check, he could be a contender for any title he chooses in WCW.

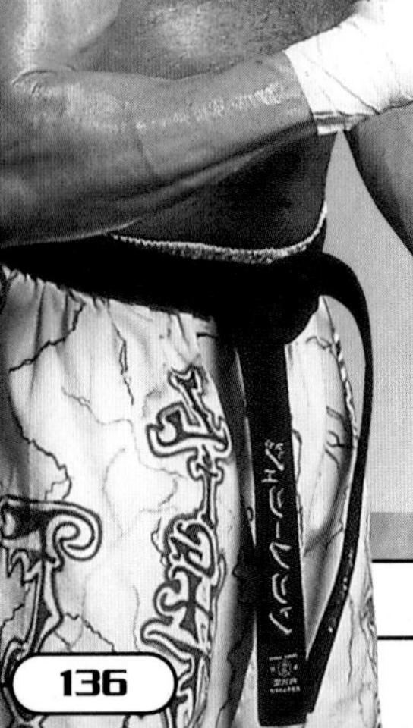

JERRY FLYNN
- Height: 6' 4"
- Weight: 250 lbs.
- Hometown: Florida
- Debut: 1991
- Finishing Maneuver: Crescent Kick

MENG

From the island of Tonga comes one of the most feared men ever to set foot in a ring. Championship belts mean nothing to him, and on the few occasions when he's had title opportunities, he was usually disqualified for some act of brutality. That should tell you all you need to know about Meng, who is as fierce and ferocious as any gladiator in the squared circle. At 6 feet tall, and just under 300 pounds, Meng throws his opponents around like rag dolls, only to shock them with kicks and karate thrusts faster than most men half his size. His natural ability, complimented by his knowledge of several forms of combat, make him an extremely well-rounded competitor and a sure champion—if he could harness his rage and aggression.

If you want to know how tough Meng is, just ask other wrestlers. Any one of the big tough men in the WCW locker room will tell you (off the record, of course) that the one man they fear most is Meng. There are plenty of stories of Meng taking care of problems with hotheaded people outside the ring!

FLAIR'S HENCHMENG

Meng's tenacity and ability have made him quite a lot of money over the years and have also given him a vaunted reputation. He's been hired several times to act as a bodyguard, and he also comes in handy as a "hired gun" to take care of potential problems for wrestlers and managers. When he was WCW President, Ric Flair was fond of booking Meng as the opponent for any wrestler that gave the Nature Boy any trouble!

DEATH GRIP

Meng is the sole master of the dreaded Tongan Death Grip, a move that once locked on is almost impossible to break. Using his speed and hand strength, Meng darts his hand under an opponent's chin, grabbing a hold on the pressure point above the throat. Squeezing on the nerve, it's only a matter of time until the opponent, unable to respond, is rendered unconscious or has his shoulder pinned to the mat.

Several managers, most notably Jimmy Hart, have tried to focus Meng in an effort to claim some wrestling glory, but inevitably, Meng's natural instinct to destroy takes over. He is tailor-made for WCW's Hardcore division, though he doesn't really need the weapons that others choose to bring to such bouts. His hands and feet are far more devastating, and his unusually hard head can withstand almost any type of blow, bash or battering. After many years in this sport, no one has been able to keep him down for long, even after hitting him with everything, including a kitchen sink!

MENG
- Height: 6' 1"
- Weight: 300 lbs.
- Home: Tonga
- Birthday: Feb. 3
- Debut: 1977
- Finishing maneuver: Tongan Death Grip

BODYSLAM

The bodyslam is a deceptive maneuver, both in execution and effect. When lifting your opponent, you must swivel his body in midair and throw out when you release him, otherwise he's liable to land on his feet or knees, and be in a perfect position to attack you. Strength is required against a large opponent, but by properly positioning your body, you can use leverage to lift wrestlers who far outweigh you. Of course, the bodyslam becomes even more effective when you throw your own weight on top of the opponent as he lands, forcing him to become the filling in a mat sandwich; this is known as a powerslam.

The Cat

Ernest Miller entered WCW in 1997 as a subdued karate master, speaking softly in interviews and carrying himself very seriously in the ring. Then, something changed. First the nickname "The Cat" was added to his introduction. Then the trunks got a little flashier, as did the clothes Ernest wore outside the ring. Soon, he started to talk a little more, bragging about his extensive karate background. Then he started bragging about his dancing skills. Soon he sounded like a cross between Muhammad Ali and a stand-up comedian, declaring "Somebody call my mama, because I'm about to whup somebody!" We're not sure where this attitude came from, but Ernest wants it all, and he wants it now!

The Cat

- **Height: 6' 2"**
- **Weight: 235 lbs.**
- **Hometown: Atlanta, GA**
- **Debut: 1997**
- **Finishing maneuver: Thrust Kick**
- **Phrase: "I am the greatest"**

Ernest Miller's versatility in the ring has been one of the key ingredients of his success in WCW. When faced with a superior grappler, he relies on his karate skills. Put him in the ring with a fellow martial artist, and he switches to his mat skills, honed from hours of working in WCW's Power Plant. This amazing versatility gives The Cat a great advantage over less gifted opponents.

Along with the Disco Inferno and Norman Smiley, Ernest is another WCW competitor who likes to celebrate in the ring with a little rhythm. His dancing skills are almost as polished as his ring skills, and the fancy footwork he displays makes you wonder if Ernest missed another possible career opportunity. Once the bell rings though, he's all business until the match is over. Then it's time to hit the music and dance some more, to the delight of the fans!

Certain people, namely the Maestro, refused to believe that Ernest was friends with the Godfather of Soul, James Brown. When told to put up or shut up, The Cat came through, bringing out the Rock'n'Roll Hall of Famer during *Superbrawl 2000*. Brown and Miller danced away to the thunderous cheers of the fans, while the disbelieving Maestro fainted! Brown even bestowed upon Miller one of his trademark capes, and in true James Brown fashion, Miller shrugged it off and kept on dancing!

Cat Fight

When The Cat gets on the microphone and declares himself a three-time world karate champion, he's not just a boasting. He truly is one of the finest practitioners of karate in the world, having won the Atomix Open Karate Tournament in Atlanta, Georgia from 1996 through 1998. In fact, it was at these tournaments that WCW officials first recognized his tremendous talent and brought him to the world of professional wrestling. Having accomplished all there was in karate, Ernest took them up on the offer of a new challenge.

Hugh Morrus

Wrestling has more than its share of strange characters, certainly more than any other sport. However, truth be told, most of them are only playing a role, doing outlandish things to garner attention for themselves. In a business with so many skilled competitors vying for glory, it's only natural that some will do anything to grab the spotlight. These are just normal people looking to gain an edge by doing crazy things. Then, there's people like Hugh Morrus. In a politically correct world, he would be referred to as mentally disturbed. In layman's terms, he's nuts.

Hugh Morrus
- **Height: 6' 2"**
- **Weight: 310 lbs.**
- **Hometown: Titusville, FL**
- **Debut: 1990**
- **Finishing maneuver: Moonsault**
- **Phrase: "Hahaha!"**

Flexible Giant

Over six feet tall and 300 pounds, and he does moonsaults? Impossible, you say! Not for Hugh Morrus, who, in addition to being born a little off-center, was also blessed with natural athletic ability. He has uncanny balance and stands on the top rope as easily as if he were standing on the ground. Hurling himself into a full backflip, when Hugh Morrus squashes his opponent, it's lights out time. He calls it No Laughing Matter, and for those on the receiving end of it, the title rings true.

Table Time

It would seem that Hugh Morrus has a love of tables, particularly the folding banquet tables that WCW uses in its dressing room area. He'll often take one into the ring, or even stow one under it for later use. He'll set it up during a match, even though he knows he's risking disqualification, and try to moonsault his opponent through it. Usually though, he'll end up with no target, as the opponent rolls out of the way, and Morrus ends up hitting nothing but wood!

If you need any proof that this man is not playing with a full deck, just look at his appearance. He wears tights with laughing faces or question marks on them. In an interview, he'll make a serious point, laugh maniacally, or speak gibberish. When he gets in the ring, however, he thrashes his opponents with no regard for his adversary or himself. The kind who sees nothing wrong in taking three punches just to land one, Morrus is a difficult opponent to prepare for.

It's hard to imagine anyone controlling Hugh Morrus, but Jimmy Hart, who has a lot of experience dealing with unstable superstars, included Morrus in his First Family. A cornerstone of the group, Morrus became somewhat of a protector to the rest of the stable, interfering in matches and making sure that the Family always came out on top of whatever battle they were embroiled in.

PAY-PER-VIEWS

Once a month, WCW holds its pay-per-view spectaculars. These are the pinnacles of the business, the shows where only the true stars get to participate. When a wrestler competes on a pay-per-view, with the whole world watching, he knows he's made it. Some of the events, like *Starrcade*, have been around since 1983, when they were broadcast in theaters and arenas around the world on closed-circuit television. With the advent of cable and satellite television, the shows are beamed into the living rooms of fans everywhere. *Halloween Havoc*, *The Great American Bash*, *SuperBrawl*, and *Spring Stampede* are just some of the mega-events that WCW holds each year in its monthly showcase of the finest wrestling in the world.

BAM
WILD

Dorling Kindersley

LONDON, NEW YORK, SYDNEY, DELHI, PARIS
MUNICH, and JOHANNESBURG

SENIOR EDITOR Jon Richards
PROJECT ART EDITOR Rob Perry
ASSOCIATE EDITOR David John
DESIGNERS Jennifer Bottomley & Guy Harvey
MANAGING ART EDITOR Cathy Tincknell
US EDITOR Margaret Parrish
DTP DESIGNER Andrew O'Brien
PRODUCTION Nicola Torode

First American Edition, 2000
00 01 02 03 04 05 10 9 8 7 6 5 4 3 2 1
Published in the United States by Dorling Kindersley Publishing, Inc.
95 Madison Avenue, New York, New York 10016

Library of Congress Cataloging-in-Publication Data

World championship wrestling: the ultimate guide.-- 1st American ed.
p. cm.

Summary: An illustrated overview of world championship wrestling including the stats, honors, and trademark maneuvers of a variety of well-known wrestlers.

ISBN 0-7894-6673-2 (hardcover)
1. Wrestling--Juvenile literature. [1. Wrestling.] I. Dorling Kindersley Publishing, Inc.
GV1195.3 .W67 2000
796.812'3--dc21
00-023238

Reproduced by Mullis Morgan, UK

Printed and bound by World Color, USA

Acknowledgements
Dorling Kindersley would like to thank Chelsea Reeves, Joseph Lester, and Lisa Pearl at WCW, and Wally Cabrera, Liza Greenwald, and Evelyn Caceres at Leisure Concepts Incorporated.